PREACHING FUNERALS

PREACHING FUNERALS

NICOLE D. McDONALD

FOREWORD BY
Frank A. Thomas

The Pilgrim Press
1300 East 9th Street
Cleveland, Ohio 44114
thepilgrimpress.com

Published 2026.

Library of Congress Cataloging-in-Publication Data on file.
LCCN: 2026936980

ISBN 978-0-8298-0841-4 (paper)
ISBN 978-0-8298-2347-9 (ebook)

Printed on acid-free paper in the United States of America.

Printed in The United States of America.

CONTENTS

FOREWORD

As I head toward the end of my full-time Christian ministry, I reflect on all the preaching that I have done. My most favorite and meaningful preaching was eulogies and funeral sermons, now that I have learned the very helpful distinction drawn and illustrated by Nicole McDonald in this very helpful resource. Eulogies and funeral sermons were the favorite part of my preaching ministry because in the setting of a deceased loved one, people seemed to be more attentive and open to listening to the message. Death is such an existential crisis for us all—either separation from a loved one in all of its expansive ramifications or secret and hidden fears of our own death regardless of how near or far we perceive it to be. The inescapable reality of death permeates the air and the question is: Is there any hope?

It was my favorite because the needs of the family were ever before me. My compassion kicks in big time when I see the mourning faces in the front row, where the tears fall like gentle rain sometimes, and other times like a thunder storm and drenching rain. Sometimes I have come in exhausted, weary, and out of strength, but when I see and feel the broken spirits and heavy hearts—the raw need for hope in front of me—with the power of God, I kick myself in gear. For the text in

Romans 10 says, "How can they believe in the God of hope whom they have not heard? And how can they hear without a preacher?" I give my very best to proclaim the gospel of the God of hope.

It is at the intersection of the needs of the family, community, etc. and the desire as a representative of the God of hope to minister to the need that this book speaks to. For those preachers who are willing to admit that even after years of preaching they could get better in the interest of helping people. And for those who are starting out and are unsure of the why, what, and how of preaching funeral sermons and eulogies, much can be gained without residing in the school of hard knocks. Every preacher needs this book on their shelves.

After over forty-five years of ministry, I am still looking forward to reading this book. Although I no longer am a pastor, and am a retired seminary professor, every now and then I am asked to preach a funeral sermon or eulogy. I want to still get better for the people who entrust me with preaching a word of hope at the hour of their most critical need and the God of hope who called me to preach in the first place.

One more thing: I am deeply appreciative of Nicole McDonald for recognizing and offering the valuable nuance of preaching the services of someone the preacher does not know. This is a unique skillset and has taken my preparation for these occurrences to another whole level. Thank you Nicole McDonald. You have done a great service to preachers everywhere and all of the people that will be helped by the quality preaching.

With eternal gratitude,

Frank A. Thomas

INTRODUCTION

Having attended hundreds of funerals over my thirteen years as a hospice chaplain, I've heard all kinds of sermons. Some sermons brought me to tears because they were so moving with expressions of love. As I listened to other sermons, I thought to myself, "What in the world is this preacher saying?" One particularly memorable funeral service served as the impetus for this book and heavily influenced my research methodology on eulogies.[1] The funeral was for a beloved choir director and church organist of a United Methodist Church. This lady, "Betty," battled many illnesses, but the most significant was Alzheimer's disease. Throughout her career as a choir director at her local United Methodist Church, Betty served two senior pastors and a third pastor was serving the church at the time of her death.

All three pastors spoke at Betty's funeral. Pastor A was the pastor that was assigned to the church early in Betty's choir directing career. He shared his positive interactions with Betty as an African American pastor in a predominately white congregation. Also, he talked about *Bonanza* and its horses for a long period of time. I have never seen *Bonanza* on television. For me, not being from the area or having lived in the period in which he was referencing, I did not connect with

Pastor A. However, many older persons in the gathered community connected with Pastor A. Some of them were parishioners when he was the pastor and others were familiar with *Bonanza*.

If we assess the sermon using Brad Braxton's writings on eulogies, Pastor A accomplished too little by focusing more on the life of the deceased than on God.[2] What he offered were words of reflection rather than a eulogy or a funeral sermon. He did not present the image of God within the life of the deceased. The correlation between the details of her life and her qualities that point to God was not evident to me. And he did not focus on a Gospel message of hope, but rather on the personal narrative of his relationship with the deceased.

The second preacher, Pastor B, was the previous pastor of the church and had sung in one of the church choirs that Betty directed prior to her illness. Pastor B's eulogy was masterful in the way in which she highlighted the Gospel and captured the essence of Betty. She captivated the congregation by singing stanzas of Betty's favorite hymns and referencing Betty's notorious one liners that made the entire congregation laugh. I don't remember the specific words of Pastor B, but I remember wishing I had met Betty prior to her Alzheimer's illness.

The third preacher, Pastor C, was the pastor of the church during the time of Betty's later stages of Alzheimer's disease and her subsequent death. Preacher C preached a funeral sermon without referencing the life of the deceased in any substantial manner. He didn't have a chance of holding anyone's attention due to the great eulogy from Pastor B and the considerable time that had already elapsed since the beginning of the service. I only remember him saying that he did not have the opportunity to meet Betty prior to her illness but that he had made several pastoral visits in the facility with Betty and her husband. I do not remember anything else Pastor C said. However, I do remember I kept looking at my watch because time was of the essence. The funeral was running long due to the three separate sermons.

These three preachers demonstrated the three types of words spoken by clergy at funerals. The first preacher gave words of reflection that focused too much on the life of the deceased and not on God. The second preacher gave a eulogy that presented the image of God within the life of the deceased in a manner that gives hope to the grieving gathered community by affirming the witness of Christ for those that believe in the Gospel. The third preacher delivered a funeral sermon that left out the life of the deceased and focused only on the Gospel message of hope. Hearing these three United Methodist pastors within the same ministerial setting sparked my interest in better understanding funeral preaching.

Betty's funeral showed that the relationship clergy has with the deceased matters significantly in the content of the sermon. As a hospice chaplain, I rarely have the luxury of drawing on a longstanding relationship with the deceased and their family. Therefore, I have to use pastoral care techniques to learn about the life of their loved one. Sometimes I am able to have one or two pastoral visits with a coherent patient prior to death. I usually have limited bereavement visits with family and friends. The information gathered through the pastoral visits allows me to develop a eulogy that presents the image of God within the life of the deceased and gives hope to the grieving gathered community by affirming the witness of Christ for those that believe in the Gospel. I wholeheartedly believe this is the task of the eulogist, regardless of one's relationship with the deceased.

I've attended too many funerals where the eulogist said, "I do not know the deceased, so I'm going to just preach Jesus." Ignoring the deceased can be hurtful to the gathered community. I've heard family members say angrily, "That preacher didn't say anything about my Momma!" Other times, the family gives the eulogist grace for not knowing their loved one.

As far as I know, I've been able to avoid causing additional pain for the grieving family. It's not because I've known the deceased. It's because I've been able to develop meaningful eulogies based on my pastoral care skills during the bereavement visits. In this book, I pass along what I've learned over the years. I hope that after reading this book and applying these techniques, you never have to tell the family, "I never met your loved one." I believe if you learn these tools and give yourself time for a meaningful bereavement visit, you will be able to preach eulogy for someone you do not know well.

Even though preaching funerals for people unknown to the clergy is a common occurrence, I have not found any resources to assist clergy in this particular endeavor. Therefore, in this book, I teach the pastoral care skills and homiletical techniques I use to preach eulogies for people I do not know well. As the methodology for this project began to unfold, I asked myself, "Is preaching a funeral sermon that ignores the life of the deceased unjust?" From a theological justice perspective, my answer is yes. Preaching a sermon during a Christian funeral that ignores the life of the deceased and does not connect the life of the deceased with the Gospel is unjust. As a chaplain, I believe in justice-oriented care that recognizes everyone was born in the *imago Dei*, the image of God. The task of a Christian funeral is to demonstrate the ways in which the deceased's life exemplified the image of God. The deceased deserves the justice a eulogist can offer by honoring the ways their life represents the Gospel.

Preaching is no stranger to justice, especially within the African American context of prophetic preaching. In *Where Have All the Prophets Gone?,* Marvin McMickle defines prophetic preaching as preaching that illuminates the wider dimensions of the gospel, God's demand for righteousness and justice, and the ways in which the Christian community obscures them.[3] McMickle believes that the task of the preacher is to keep the focus on communal injustices through the word of prophetic preaching. The concept of prophetic preaching led me to another question of justice: "Can eulogies represent examples of prophetic preaching?" Again, my answer is yes. There are plenty of historical prophetic eulogies within African American preaching, such as the Rev. Dr. Joseph Lowery's eulogy of Coretta Scott King, the Rev. Dr. Al Sharpton's eulogy of Michael Brown, and the Rev. Dr. Martin Luther King, Jr.'s eulogy of three of the four little girls killed in the Sixteenth Street Baptist Church bombing. All of these eulogies focus on God's demand for righteousness while identifying the ways in which the United States of America perpetuates injustice.

The irony of a prophetic eulogy is that most scholars provide clear distinctions between prophetic and pastoral preaching. Historically, Black church homiletics minimized pastoral preaching while emphasizing the prophetic function of preaching. In Chapter 8 of the book *Black Church Studies*, the late Dale P. Andrews attributes the emphasis on prophetic preaching to the urgent demands of justice for the African American community in America. Due to injustice, "the assaults of racism, slavery, Jim and Jane Crow, and 'un-civil rights' raised a false split between the challenge of pastoral care as nurturing wholeness and prophetic care as seeking justice."[4] I agree with Andrews regarding the false split between pastoral and prophetic. I think all preaching should be characterized as pastoral, in the sense that all preaching addresses the needs of the gathered community. Addressing these needs sometimes sounds like prophetic preaching that calls out injustice while imagining a future reflective of God's love for all creation. At other times, addressing these needs involves priestly preaching that may emphasize the sacraments or doctrine. And yet, the gathered community may need a sermon encouraging emotional intelligence of compassion, empathy, and communal love reflective of pastoral care.

In this book, I narrow the gap of the distinctions between pastoral and prophetic preaching by arguing that preaching a eulogy for someone unknown is an act of prophetic proclamation. A eulogy can be pastoral by comforting the gathered community and prophetic by seeking justice for the Christian witness of the deceased. In Chapter 1, I contextualize hospice chaplaincy in light of preaching funerals of people unknown to the eulogist. Based on my professional experience, I expand our understanding of funeral preaching by redefining key terms like funeral sermon and eulogy. The chapter concludes with a discussion of prophetic eulogies and an analysis of the Rev. Dr. Martin Luther King Jr.'s eulogy of three of the four girls killed in the Birmingham church bombing in 1963. In the next chapter, I survey the foundational scholarship on Christian funeral preaching, whose insights I use to develop eulogies for people I do not know well. The survey emphasizes African American preaching. At the end of Chapter 2, I demonstrate the application of the scholarship by providing an analysis of a eulogy I delivered for a patient I did not know well. In Chapter 3, I evaluate interviews of pastors and other clergy with experience eulogizing people they do not know well to determine best practices. In Chapter 4, I introduce the methods I use for developing eulogies for people unknown to the eulogist. Additionally, I provide examples of eulogies I delivered using these methods. I conclude with a summary of what I've learned during the development of this book and with a copy of the eulogy I preached for my beloved Aunt Anne. Anne Mae Morse died unexpectedly in May 2025. Her eulogy is an example of several methods demonstrated in this book, even though I knew her well. Ultimately, the concepts presented in this book can be used to develop eulogies for any and every one, known and unknown to the eulogist.

CHAPTER **ONE**

CONTEXT MATTERS

As a hospice chaplain, I visit the homes of patients who, according to their doctor's prognosis, have six months or less to live. Sometimes the patient comes onto our hospice service and lives one week, and other times they live one year. I usually have at least two to three chaplaincy visits prior to the patient's death. If the patient suffers from dementia or another form of cognitive impairment, I visit the family and call frequently to provide intentional emotional and spiritual support to those closest to the patient.

During the initial visit, I complete a comprehensive assessment of the person's spiritual life to gather general information about their denominational affiliation, church membership, and the like. I attempt to understand the ways in which the patient connects spiritually so that I can determine how best to meet their spiritual needs. Typically, I spend time educating the patient and family about the role of the chaplain, so they do not confuse the chaplain's responsibilities with those of a church pastor.

I explain that I am available to support their spiritual and emotional needs. I do not visit with an agenda to evangelize or judge their lack of participation in church. Furthermore, I explain that I visit patients representing the entire spiritual spectrum, from religious persons who attend church every Sunday to spiritual persons who meet God in nature. If they would like Bible study, we can read and study God's word. If they want someone to talk to about life, sports, or the news, we can do that as well. In my experience, regardless of religion, patients welcome companionship during their time of illness.

If the patient accepts chaplain visitation, I visit their residence, listen to their concerns, respond to questions about death and dying, pray, read scripture, and overall, just meet them where they are spiritually and emotionally. I seek to be a non-anxious, non-judgmental presence and to convey acceptance with not only my words, but my body language as well. My goal for the chaplain visit is to meet the spiritual and emotional needs of my patients, regardless of race, sexual orientation, gender, spirituality, and religion.

As the chaplain, I attend funerals on behalf of the hospice organization. I officiate the funerals for some of my hospice patients, especially those without any church affiliation. Usually, I am the last clergy member the family encounters before the patient's death, which is why some families ask me to officiate the funeral. As the officiant, I act as the worship leader and speak words of comfort in the form of a funeral sermon or a eulogy.

Thus far, there have been very few people for whom I could not develop a eulogy. One example was a patient I met once prior to her death. I met the patient and her boyfriend at her home. During this visit, the patient was indifferent towards chaplain visitation because she didn't think she was dying anytime soon. The patient died less than two weeks later. After her death, the boyfriend was in such grief that he could not talk to me about his girlfriend. I called the woman's best friend and she couldn't talk to me either. Neither had the fortitude to engage in the life review process by reflecting on the life of their beloved friend. I did not gather enough information about the life of the deceased in order to develop a eulogy. Therefore, I preached a funeral sermon that offered a Gospel message of hope to the gathered community.

In another example, I received one of the best compliments after a eulogy which was, "I could tell you knew him very well." I put my foot in my mouth by clarifying, "I never met him. By the time he came to our service, he was already in a coma." Even though I did not know the deceased, my job was to capture the essence of his being by telling his story in conjunction with the Gospel. I "got to know" the deceased during my visits with his wife.

I met the deceased's wife during my initial visit and listened to her story for an hour. She grew up in a Methodist church and he was Catholic, but neither were active members in any denominational church. The day before he died, I sat by his bedside with his wife for approximately five hours reviewing his life. With these two encounters, I was able to capture his biography and their love story to develop a sermon that presented the details of the life of the deceased as the "good word" that connected the grief of the mourners to the promises of Christ. [1]

I had another encounter with a patient's spouse who asked me to "do" the service of her dying husband. They were unchurched and spiritual. They rejected organized religion and had faith in God that was characterized by prayer and love. The widow knew she wanted Christian clergy to organize the funeral, preach the eulogy, and conduct a brief graveside service. However, she was not aware of the correct terminology, such as officiate, eulogist, and graveside committal.

The patient was on our hospice service for two months. In those months, I met the entire family for the chaplain's initial spiritual comprehensive assessment and visited with the husband and wife one more time prior to his death. After the patient's death, I sat with the widowed wife, trying to get an understanding of her expectations of the funeral service. The only pertinent information she could express was that during her grandfather's funeral the preacher recited a passage from scripture about walking through valleys of death. She wanted to make sure I read that scripture because it meant so much to her. The woman did not know she was referring to the twenty-third Psalm.

These encounters support the findings of the "Pew Forum on Religion and Public Life" study published in February 2025. The Pew Research Center conducted similar surveys in 2007, 2014, and 2023-2024, with each demonstrating a decline in religious affiliation in the United States. According to the study, "the number of people who say they are unaffiliated with any particular faith today (29%) which is an increase from the results in 2014 of (22.8%) equaling approximately 56 million."[2] Fifty-six million is roughly 19 million more than was reported in the similar survey taken in 2007.[3] These statistics, specifically within the Protestant denominations, are increasing yearly. However, the decline in religious affiliation does not necessarily equate to a decline in Christian spirituality. Generally, people retain individual faith practices, such as prayer, without being part of organized religion. With the decline in organized religion, more Christian clergy will find themselves in situations of preaching funerals for people they do not know. In order to address the phenomena, this book analyzes the ways in which clergy develop funeral sermons and eulogies for people with whom we have brief ministerial relationships.

The Funeral of Someone Unknown to Clergy[4]

Christian clergy often preach funerals for people they do not know, such as parishioners' relatives who are disconnected from the church, unaffiliated community members, soldiers who are not active in their unit's spiritual life, or hospice patients without church affiliations. These individuals, though not part of a religious community at the time of their death, identify as Christians and desire a Christian funeral. Their expectation creates a dilemma: *how do clergy honor the faith of someone who identified as Christian but lived outside the faith community?*[5]

Typically, clergy honor the faith of the deceased in the form of a sermon, either a funeral sermon or eulogy. The terms funeral sermon and eulogy are often used interchangeably in writings. However, they are not the same, and understanding the distinction will be important as you read on. In *Preaching Words: 144 Key Terms in Homiletics*, John McClure defines the funeral sermon as a sermon on the occasion of a funeral.[6] He states the twofold purpose of the funeral sermon as 1) to help the family members and friends confront the reality of the death of a loved one; and 2) to offer comfort and hope. For the Christian funeral, the funeral sermon is a reminder that "through our baptism we are being translated into a new life that is not our own, but resurrection life given to us in and through Jesus Christ."[7] McClure criticizes the cultural push for the funeral sermon to become a eulogy by focusing on biographical and narrative embellishments. He suggests incorporating information of the deceased's life within the proclamation of the Gospel.

Thomas Long, in *Accompany Them with Singing: The Christian Funeral*, characterizes the funeral sermon in light of the historical function of the Christian funeral as a symbolic piece of drama, walking the deceased on the last mile of the journey toward resurrection.[8] Therefore, the Christian funeral sermon (not a eulogy focusing on the deceased) must be biblical and contextual. Additionally, the funeral sermon must proclaim a message of hope for those in the congregation and the fellowship of believers. Long states that the funeral sermon is not a eulogy. He also mentions that the contemporary funeral sermon would be sterile and strange if it did not mention the life of the deceased.

Peter M. Wherry, in *Preaching Funerals in the Black Church: Bringing Perspective to Pain*, uses funeral sermon and eulogy interchangeably due to their mutual inclusivity. However, Wherry distinguishes the eulogy from the funeral sermon. The eulogy presents the details of the life of the deceased as the "good word" that connects the grief of the mourners to the promises of Christ for those that believe in the Gospel. Wherry notes that eulogies may be preached for persons that the preacher knows intimately. He quotes Brad Braxton to elaborate on the development of a eulogy. Braxton writes,

> While a eulogy can attempt to do too much, it can also accomplish too little. A eulogy that accomplishes too little focuses more on the life of the deceased than on God. We derive the word "eulogy" from Greek words that mean "good word." Primarily, a eulogy should present the "good word" of God's presence, actions, and promises. Effective eulogies sensitively seek to include significant details from the life of the deceased. Yet, a eulogy's ultimate aim is to situate the life of the deceased and the hurt and hope of the mourners within the eternal framework of God's gospel.[9]

My working definition of a eulogy is as follows: *a eulogy presents the image of God within the life of the deceased in a manner that gives hope to the grieving gathered community by affirming the witness of Christ for those who believe in the Gospel.* This definition captures the three-fold purpose of a eulogy: comforting the grieving community, honoring the life of the deceased, and presenting the Gospel. Additionally, my working definition of a funeral sermon is a Gospel message of hope that comforts the gathered community by addressing the reality of the death of a loved one.[10]

"Typically, the type of sermon preached for the deceased within the faith community is a eulogy, presumably because the clergy has firsthand knowledge of the details of the life of the deceased."[11] A funeral sermon is preached by the clergy if the deceased is unknown. Based on the working definitions outlined above, the eulogy honors the deceased by describing how the deceased's life exuded Christian characteristics, i.e., the image of God, while the funeral sermon focuses on the Gospel message of hope and forgoes the details of the deceased's life. Thus, the funeral sermon marginalizes the faith of the deceased by ignoring their Christian witness, and thereby assigns them an unimportant status within the Christian community.

I attended a funeral of a well-known man in a close-knit community. He was a man who was in and out of the streets, but lived for God in the latter years of his life. The clergy that preached the funeral was the deceased's mother's pastor. This African American Baptist pastor had been in ministry for over fifty years. This pastor preached a phenomenal funeral sermon, classic Black Baptist, old school preaching with three points and a whoop. As a preacher, I loved the pastor's funeral sermon. He preached Jesus with conviction, clarity, and charisma. The sermonic text was taken from Luke 7:11–18 where Jesus raises the widow's son from the dead during the funeral procession. The point of departure was biblical, but it was from the pastor's point of contact, the deceased's mother. As a mourner of the deceased who was my patient, I asked myself, "What about this man's faith journey?" The deceased's life is a testament to God's grace and mercy. The powerful testimony of his faith journey was not acknowledged in the funeral sermon.

Marginalizing the life and faith of the deceased is unjust. The eulogy is an act of prophetic proclamation that redeems the value of the deceased by revealing their Christian witness as a testament to their faith. "Since the details of the deceased's faith are unknown to the clergy, during the bereavement visit, clergy must employ pastoral care skills to understand the Christian witness of the deceased."[12] Independent of my relationship with the deceased, I attempt to develop a eulogy that presents the image of God within the life of the deceased in a manner that gives hope to the grieving gathered community by affirming the witness of Christ for those that believe in the Gospel. The eulogy has three aims: to comfort the grieving community, to honor the life of the deceased, and to present the Gospel message. My point of departure is always the life of the deceased. When I do not know the deceased firsthand, I provide pastoral support to the bereaved family and friends in order to hear the deceased's faith for the development of the eulogy.[13]

Prophetic Eulogies

As I turn to the Rev. Dr. Martin Luther King, Jr.'s eulogy of three of the four girls killed in the 16th Street Baptist Church bombing, I want to provide some context. During the height of the Civil Rights Movement, the Klu Klux Klan bombed this Black church on Sunday, September 15, 1963 in Birmingham, Alabama. The congregants were preparing for worship for Youth Day and the young children were in Sunday School.[14] For the analysis, I want to acknowledge several assumptions. I assume that King did not know the girls or their families. Even though he was unfamiliar with the families, King was tasked with the eulogy due to his leadership in the Civil Rights Movement. Therefore, I assume he or someone from his team either had a bereavement visit or a bereavement phone call with the families.

In this eulogy, King's posture is both pastoral, in that he comforts the gathered community, and prophetic, in that he situates the killings within the larger Civil Rights Movement. King observes the three aims of a eulogy: to comfort the gathered community, to honor the life of the deceased, and to present the Gospel. He comforts the family and honors the life of the girls who were murdered. The presentation of the Gospel is a message of equality and justice rooted in the Civil Rights Movement. This eulogy remains grounded in the message of God's justice, and it adheres to the working definition of a eulogy that presents the image of God within the life of the deceased in a manner that gives hope to the grieving gathered community by affirming the witness of Christ for those that believe in the Gospel.

The context of the Civil Rights Movement heavily shaped the content of the eulogy. The first half of the eulogy has a tone of righteous indignation that calls out individual and collective evil in an American society riddled with hatred and racism. King describes the bombing as "one of the most vicious and tragic crimes ever perpetrated against humanity."[15] He calls out the ways in which several parties contribute to the systematic sin of racism in America, including the federal government, right-wing northern Republicans, ministers, and African Americans. King identifies the children as "martyred heroines of a holy crusade for freedom and human dignity."[16] As an offering of hope, King reframes the tragedy by imagining that "the spilled blood of these innocent girls may cause the whole citizenry of Birmingham to transform the negative extremes of a dark past into the positive extremes of a bright future. Indeed, this tragic event may cause the white South to come to terms with its conscience."[17]

Framed in the context of the battle for justice, the death of these young girls becomes a powerful image of hope during the Civil Rights Movement. Perhaps King's emphasis on the prophetic allows him to compensate for his lack of knowledge about the deceased. Even though King offers minimal details of the life of the girls, their deaths remain the focal point of the eulogy as martyrs for justice. He centers the deceased in the context of God's justice for America.

In the second half of the eulogy, King pivots to comforting the grieving family by saying, "May I now say a word to you, the members of the bereaved families?"[18] Here King focuses on the universality of death and the Christian faith that believes in eternal life. He identifies the girls' actions when they died—discussing eternal love in the church—as something the parents can be proud of. King closes the sermon with a quote from Horatio in Shakespeare's *Hamlet*. King says, "And today, as I stand over the remains of these beautiful, darling girls, I paraphrase the words of Shakespeare: Good night, sweet princesses.

Good night, those who symbolize a new day. And may the flight of angels take thee to thy eternal rest. God bless you."[19]

King's discussion of the children's lives is brief for a eulogy. Brevity may be expected when collectively honoring the lives of three individuals. King does not give many details about the individual lives of each girl. He doesn't even name the children, which is highly unusual in a eulogy. Even though King is brief, he highlights the most important aspects of the girls' shared lives; they died in the church talking about the love of God, and as martyrs they symbolize a new day.

This eulogy is an act of prophetic proclamation for two reasons. The Rev. Dr. Martin Luther King Jr., the leader of the Civil Rights Movement, did not know the three young girls. Rather than ignoring their lives, King affirms their Christian witness by detailing the ways in which their lives exemplify the Gospel. Unlike other eulogies for people unknown to clergy, the three girls were affiliated with and attended church. They were members of the religious faith community of the Sixteenth Street Baptist Church. Through the eulogy, King places the young victims of racism at the center of the Civil Rights Movement. In so doing, he etches the names of Addie Mae Collins, Carol McNair, and Cynthia Wesley into the sandstones of the Movement. Even though they were among the many killed due to racism during that time period, King's act of prophetic proclamation immortalized these three girls.

We can take a more systematic look at how King's eulogy maintains the hallmarks of prophetic preaching by applying the categories from Lenora Tubbs Tisdale's writings in *Prophetic Preaching: A Pastoral Approach*. Tisdale's seven hallmarks of prophetic preaching are as follows: demonstrates the biblical witness of Hebrew prophets and Jesus, challenges the status quo, identifies shortcomings of social order, names what is not of God and a new reality of God, offers hope of a new day, incites courage, and provides honesty about the things that break the heart of God.[20] Table 1 demonstrates how King's eulogy fulfills Tisdale's hallmarks of prophetic preaching.

Table 1: The Rev. Dr. Martin Luther King Jr.'s Eulogy for the Young Victims of the Sixteenth Street Baptist Church Bombing

Hallmark of Prophetic Preaching	Excerpts from the Eulogy[21]
Biblical witness of Hebrew prophets/Jesus	We must not become bitter, nor must we harbor the desire to retaliate with violence. No, we must not lose faith in our white brothers. Somehow, we must believe that the most misguided among them can learn to respect the dignity and the worth of all human personality.
Countercultural/ challenges status quo	They say to us that we must be concerned not merely about who murdered them, but about the system, the way of life, the philosophy which produced the murderers.
Shortcomings of social order (corporate issues)	They have something to say to a federal government that has compromised with the undemocratic practices of southern Dixiecrats and the blatant hypocrisy of right-wing northern Republicans.
Naming what is not of God and a new reality of God	They have something to say to every minister of the gospel who has remained silent behind the safe security of stained-glass windows.
Offers hope of a new day/liberation of God's oppressed people	The spilled blood of these innocent girls may cause the whole citizenry of Birmingham to transform the negative extremes of a dark past into the positive extremes of a bright future. Indeed, this tragic even may cause the white South to come to terms with its conscience.
Incites courage/ empowers work to change social order	They have something to say to every Negro who has passively accepted the evil system of segregation and who has stood on the sidelines in a mighty struggle for justice.
Honest about the things that break the heart of God	These children—unoffending, innocent, and beautiful—were the victims of one of the most vicious and tragic crimes ever perpetrated against humanity.

Tisdale's hallmarks of prophetic preaching provide guidance towards the development of a prophetic eulogy that balances the call to consciousness with hope. King's eulogy presents each hallmark and centers the deceased with the phrase, "They have something to say." Based on King's eulogy, as a preacher writing a prophetic eulogy, consider how each hallmark is applied to the context of the deceased's death. For example, the biblical witness of Jesus honors the dignity of every human, especially marginalized people. Therefore, King mentions how racist white persons can learn to respect all humanity. Humanity is not respected when we kill one another. As the leader of the non-violent movement, King admonishes violence against violence in light of respecting all humanity.

Despite the prophetic power of his eulogy, I was surprised to find that King does not use biblical scripture for the sermonic text. He mentions Isaiah 11:6, "a little child shall lead them," when he talks about the ways in which the young girls' deaths can lead the nation towards peace and equality. However, Isaiah 11:6 is not centered throughout the eulogy. The lack of centering scripture is peculiar within contemporary African American preaching. Typically, both funeral sermons and eulogies are rooted in the Bible. However, King emphasizes God's justice as a whole instead of one particular sermonic text.

Because the sermon is not focused on a scripture, I initially wanted to classify this eulogy as words of reflection. However, upon further evaluation, the eulogy gives a Gospel message without directly quoting scripture. The Gospel message is that there is hope in the Lord. No matter the despair, God is with us each and every step of the journey. The death of these three young girls was not in vain because it will inspire change in the race relations of society as well as change in the system that manifests hatred amongst the people. Ultimately, God will get the glory. Even though this eulogy does not center a biblical text, it meets the three-fold purpose of eulogies by comforting the grieving community, honoring the life of the deceased, and presenting the Gospel message. Therefore, this eulogy expands my understanding of eulogies in that a biblical text is not necessarily required.

In conclusion, King's masterful prophetic eulogy honors the Christian witness of the girls without mentioning their names or centering a Biblical scripture. King's homiletical prowess emerges in the prophetic eulogy with his poetic expressions, creativity, and imagination. King demonstrates that even in the event of a tragic injustice of murder, a preacher can develop a eulogy for someone they don't know through the integration of pastoral care and prophetic preaching tools.

In Chapter 3, I provide pastoral care techniques based on my experience along with the professional experience of ten other clergy I interviewed during the research for this book. Additionally, I use the work of two primary scholars to develop eulogies, the tenants of African American preaching described by Henry Mitchell, the Dean of African American Homiletics, and Thomas Long's eight purposes of a good funeral sermon. Their scholarship informs the substance of my eulogies that honor the Christian faith of the deceased, presents the Gospel message, and comforts the grieving gathered community. The next chapter surveys the scholarship on funeral preaching, with an emphasis on African American preaching.

CHAPTER **TWO**

SURVEY OF SCHOLARSHIP ON PREACHING FUNERALS

When I was in seminary, I took a preaching course with Rev. Nathan Dell on Special Occasion Preaching. We discussed preaching on Women's Day, Men's Day, Mother's Day, Youth Day, etc. Relative to all the special occasions we reviewed in class, our discussion of funeral preaching was minimal. However, we watched a recording of Professor Dell's eulogy of his friend and colleague, the Rev. Dr. Miles Jones. I will never forget how proud Rev. Dell was of that eulogy. Funeral preaching is a special occasion wherein the gathered community can celebrate the life that was lived and worship the God who walks with us in the valley of the shadow of death. In this chapter, I survey the existing scholarship and close by using the scholarship to analyze a eulogy I delivered for a patient I did not know well.

Contemporary Funeral Practices

In *Accompany Them with Singing: The Christian Funeral*, Thomas Long discusses the Christian funeral in light of history, biblical theology, Christology, soteriology, and eschatology, while seeking to answer two questions: What is the purpose of the Christian funeral? And how do clergy fulfill that purpose, responsibly? Long concludes that the purpose of the Christian funeral is to re-enact the Gospel script through worship; whereby, the gathered community remains hopeful in the eternal promises of the Resurrected Christ. Clergy use the holy person, a holy place, a holy people, and a holy script to direct a worshipful drama that allows the cast to collectively bring their burdens to the Lord as an offering and pick up their cross by continuing the work of Christ.

Long believes that the Christian funeral has been co-opted by commercialism, cultural trends, and sentimental views of spirituality. As a consequence, he claims that it no longer fulfills its purpose. Examples include caskets being sold at Costco, multiple speakers in lieu of a eulogy, discussions of death being considered politically incorrect, and the trend of memorials without the body, rather than a funeral displaying the dead body. He calls for the reformation of Christian funeral practices in order to regain the religious significance of the Christian funeral. The reformation of the Christian funeral practices will nourish the human spirit, strengthen the community of Christ, proclaim the gospel, remember, and honor the dead in Christ, as well as shine the light of the resurrection of hope for all to see.[1]

According to Long, the purpose of the funeral is to mark the saint's journey that began at baptism and moves along the last mile of the way, returning to God with the victory over death.[2] Long believes that the funeral sermon must proclaim a biblical and contextual message of hope. The funeral sermon is not a eulogy that focuses on the deceased, but rather a Gospel message that uplifts the congregation. However, Long also mentions that the contemporary funeral sermon would be sterile and strange if it did not mention the life of the deceased in some manner.

Long identifies eight purposes of a good funeral sermon: kerygmatic, oblational, ecclesial, therapeutic, Eucharistic, missional, commemorative, and educational. He believes each purpose should be incorporated into the funeral sermon. A brief explanation is as follows:

1. Kerygmatic – the proclamation of the gospel of the resurrected Christ
2. Oblational – bring an offering, often characterized as love for the deceased "saint"
3. Ecclesial – the communion of saints on earth as it is in heaven
4. Therapeutic – the promises of God; i.e., joy and comfort in times of grief
5. Eucharistic – gratitude for life in light of God's image and grace
6. Missional – serve the world for the Kingdom of God
7. Commemorative – faithful storytelling of the "saint"
8. Educational – teach us to number our days[3]

The incorporation of Long's eight purposes of a good funeral sermon provides depth to the eulogy, which reflects the sacredness of the special occasion of honoring life and worshiping the creator of life, God. Long does not demand that the speaker dedicate extended paragraphs to each purpose in the eulogy. Many of them can be stated simply in one sentence. More importantly, the purposes can be used to craft a eulogy that honors the relationship between the "saint," their spiritual community, and God. The spiritual community may or may not include a church or any form of organized religion. The spiritual community can be where the "saint" met God: in nature, in serving their family, in their devotion to a spouse, or even their commitment to a vocation. The purposes set a tone of cherished remembrance.

In his essay, "The African American Funeral Sermon: Divine Re-framing of Human Tragedy," Frank A. Thomas characterizes the funeral sermon as a divine reframing of human tragedy that enables people "to look at tragic and painful events and emotions, and through illumination of scripture and the presence of the Holy Spirit, one sees a truer spiritual reality."[4] The spiritual reality is the divine perspective of God that Thomas identifies as the assurance of grace. According to Thomas, the celebration is a traditional way in which the preacher invites the gathered community to experience the assurance of grace: "Celebration is the culmination of the sermonic design, where a moment is created in which the remembrance of a redemptive past and/or the conviction of a liberated future transforms the events immediately experienced."[5]

Thomas outlines the following three-step methodology for reframing the human tragedy of death in the eulogy:

1. **Step One:** Facing the reality of death – The preacher names the pain and grief.
2. **Step Two:** Applying the gospel to the bad news – The preacher applies the word of God to the situation which gives an alternative perspective and offers resolution that may take years to experience.
3. **Step Three:** Celebrating the gospel – The preacher celebrates God's word of comfort, healing, victory over death and the promises of God.

Interestingly, Thomas does not mention the inclusion of the details of the deceased's life. Therefore, I interpret Thomas as primarily referring to funeral sermons in this essay. However, in each step of Thomas's method, the preacher may incorporate specific details of the life of the deceased that reflects the image of God in order to preach a eulogy rather than a funeral sermon.

Frank Thomas's three-step methodology for reframing is similar to my working definition of a funeral sermon in that it helps grieving people face the reality of death by presenting God's word of comfort. Steps one and three are applicable to all Christian funerals and eulogies.

With regards to step two, I agree with the practice of applying the Gospel to the situation in order to give an alternative perspective. However, I caution against offering only a long-term resolution that may take years to experience.

Generally, long-term resolutions focus on the mourners' eschatology of being reunited with Christ and seeing our loved ones again in heaven. However, short-term resolutions assist the grieving process by demonstrating a progression of healing. For example, a short-term goal may be getting out of bed and going to lunch with a friend. It is important to set small achievable goals that people can experience sooner rather than later. During the bereavement period, people take one day at a time. Grief is a marathon and not a sprint.

In another essay, "*Farewell to my Father: Funeral Reflections from a 'Preacher's Kid,'*" Brad Braxton argues the primary purpose of Christian funerals is to remind the gathered community of our future with God on and off these earthly shores. Funerals serve to provide rituals of separation, facilitate the process of grieving, and assist mourners with their transition to a new phase of life.[6] Braxton believes that hope unites these three functions. He draws on Andrew Lester's definition of hope as "a trusting anticipation of the future based on an understanding of a God who is trustworthy and who calls us into an open-ended future."[7]

As Braxton prepares for funerals, he seeks to intentionally emphasize the presence of hope in the following three ways:

1. **Encourages the family to stand during the singing of hymns.** At Braxton's father's funeral, the family stood during the hymns to symbolize their souls having assumed a tiptoe posture of expectations, awaiting the sweet future available to them through their faith in God.
2. **Uses specific language on the bulletin.** On his father's bulletin, Braxton printed "May 21, 1929: The Beginning of Life – August 3, 2004: The Beginning of Life Eternal."

3. **Reminds the gathered community of the promises of God.** At the graveside, Braxton said, "Easter is God's cosmic chuckling at the presumptuousness of death." He laughed and reiterated hopefulness through God's promise of a family reunion.

Braxton advises clergy to remember that the eulogy is not the sole mediator of the gospel, implying that they do not have to be long. Typically, his eulogies are no longer than fifteen minutes. Additionally, Braxton highlights the power of rituals because they are "ceremonial symbolic actions by which people express their deepest convictions."[8] In his father's funeral, Braxton's mother placed a red rose in the casket prior to the closing, representative of his father's passion for gardening and the "Rose of Sharon" Jesus the Christ. Lastly, Braxton cautions ministers against preaching a eulogy that does too little by focusing on the life of the deceased rather than God. A good eulogy amplifies the details of the deceased's life while keeping the homiletical focus on God.

I appreciate Brad Braxton's intentionality with the ways in which he offers hope through his liturgy and use of symbols. Like Braxton, my eulogies are usually fifteen minutes or less because brevity is important during funerals. I also believe that rituals are powerful during the funeral. Sometimes they express our deepest convictions. At other times the familiarity of the rituals provides comfort to the grieving gathered community.

Experiential Encounter with the Word

In *Celebration and Experience in Preaching*, Henry Mitchell identifies three elements of a meaningful experiential encounter with the word: "a text from the Bible, encouraging trust in and obedience to the word, together with a behavioral purpose that flows from that text, enabling clear focus on the application of the text to real life; an understanding of experiential encounter, enabling identification with and into the word; and an understanding of emotion, the timing of suspense, and the role of climatic celebration, enabling ecstatic reinforcement of the text and its behavioral purpose."[9]

The Biblical "text should be chosen for clarity of behavioral purpose and memorable brevity, as well as for helpful guidance in a specific human need."[10] The behavioral purpose flows from the text, whether explicitly or implicitly. The behavior should be clearly identified in the sermon as a positive action that encourages the audience to live faithfully by trusting God and obeying that text.

The second element necessary for an experiential encounter of the word is an understanding of hearing, other senses, and how they relate to belief. The hearing experience should include vivid details and images; familiarity, identification, and vicarious experience; and homiletic moves in consciousness.[11]

Vivid details and images draw on Jesus' parables, which are succinct stories that illustrate a moral or spiritual lesson. The parables allow the hearer to understand the teachings by connecting familiarities of life with the spiritual lesson. Similar to Jesus' parables, the preacher must incorporate "authentic, historical, fill-in details that make a person, place, thing, or a whole story come to life in the mental processes and total experience of the hearer."[12]

The hearing experience should include a discussion of familiarity, identification, and vicarious experiences that help the audience relate to the Biblical text. For example, using the faith of the centurion from Luke 7:1–10, Mitchell references the centurion's rank, which translates to "top sergeant." He also suggests that the centurion could have lost his "stripes." The text does not mention rank or stripes; however, the image draws a familiar connection between the centurion's experience and that of military families. The familiar association and identification lead to vicarious experiences.[13] The association allows hearers to commit to the behavioral purpose as if they have lived through the situation within the text.

The last element of the hearing experience are homiletical moves, which Mitchell defines as "meaningful modules or groups of words and sentences that describe the images used to express in the concrete what we cannot adequately verbalize in the abstract."[14] Moves are the sermonic points. Mitchell differentiates between moves and points, writing that, "points are made to score in the intellect while moves involve the whole person in experiential encounters of body, strength, emotion, intuition, mental processes and spirit."[15]

In theory, the difference between a move and a point seems abstract; however, in practice, during the preaching moment, you know the difference. When a preacher incorporates homiletical moves, the listeners have encounters with the word. These encounters may include reflection on certain experiences that relate to the preached word. Whether it be joy, sorrow, or grief, the encounter is a moment of resonance for the listeners, who can say, "That preacher is talking to me!" Homiletical moves tap into sacred memory and the embodied hope of the not yet, whereas points produce only intellectual curiosity for the listeners to consider and not experience.

The last component necessary for an experiential encounter of the word is an understanding of emotion, the timing of suspense, and climactic celebration. Mitchell insists that feelings require a means of passionate expression derived from the personal conviction of the preacher that authentically translates to the hearers during the sermon. Power lies in the crescendo of the deep feelings in the homiletic discipline called "timing of impact." The intensity of emotions escalates from a low-key rising of a dramatic conflict to a peak intensity and then resolution.[16] The sermon ends with the climatic celebration of the text and its purpose.

While Mitchell's work does not specifically relate to funeral preaching, he reminds us that creativity and imagery are required for good, experiential preaching. I believe that imagination is one of the hallmarks of some of the best eulogies I've ever heard. I once heard the Rev. Dr. Thomasine Reid, the first woman pastor of the historic Union Baptist Church in Virginia Beach, Virginia preach a masterful eulogy of someone who loved the color blue. After that eulogy, I understood that the color blue was from God and God alone. Pastor Reid's eulogy was so inspirational that I wanted to wear the color blue the rest of the week.

Additional Strategies[17]

Three homiletic approaches I believe are particularly useful for preaching funerals are the character sketch, dialectic preaching, and inductive preaching. Henry Mitchell, Peter Wherry, and John McClure provide helpful guidance for the use of these approaches. The character sketch is a genre of preaching that combines biblical data and other materials to bring to full, living proportions a character from the Bible.[18] To develop a character sketch, the preacher chooses a biblical figure who has similar traits to the deceased. The preacher gathers small narratives to illustrate the trait to with listeners. These traits should represent Christian morals and values that are worthy of emulation. Based on the connection with the biblical character and the deceased, the listeners are compelled to incorporate that trait into their own lives.[19]

Mitchell recommends applying the character sketch to abstract or general text, such as 1 Thessalonians 5:18, on giving thanks in everything. He suggests using biblical persons, such as Paul, David, or Abraham, to bring to life the principle of giving thanks. Mitchell implies that the character sketch is a "best practice" approach for funeral sermons or eulogies. As a pastor preparing for a funeral, he chose biblical texts that embodied the characteristics reflective in the life of the deceased person.

Dialectic preaching is a sermonic method with a thematic focus that contrasts the ideal situation with reality.[20] Peter M. Wherry identifies dialectic preaching as one of the most useful methods for preaching funerals for a person who died under questionable circumstances, such as a murder or drug overdose. Dialectic preaching works well for the death of a child because it contrasts the ideal situation of a child growing up to be an adult with the reality of the death. The late Samuel DeWitt Proctor outlines the key components of the dialectic method of preaching:

1. **Proposition:** the sermon summarized in a sentence or two.
2. **Subject:** essentially, the sermon title.
3. **Thesis:** a statement of an ideal or desired conditions; describes how life should be. (This often functions as the introduction to a sermon.)
4. **Antithesis:** a statement of the real condition; serves as a counterpart to the thesis and highlights the obstacles in attaining the ideal. (This may be included as part of the introduction.)
5. **Relevant Question:** a doorway to the body of the sermon creates a "need to know" in the minds of the hearers.
6. **Synthesis:** encompassed in the body of the sermon; it answers the relevant question and bridges the gap between ideal and real.[21]

Finally, inductive preaching is a form of preaching in which the preacher delays the full statement of the sermon's theme or idea.[22] In *Preaching Words: 144 Key Terms in Homiletics*, McClure attributes the popularity of inductive preaching to Fred Craddock, who believes the preacher and listeners travel together towards insight within the preaching experience. "According to McClure, the preacher's subject weaves through stories and images that invite the listeners to resonate with the shared experiences, leading up to the sermon's theme."[23] The insight is often ambiguous allowing the preacher to leave the sermon open-ended for the listeners to make their own connections and conclusions.[24]

In *Preaching Funerals in the Black Church: Bringing Perspective to Pain*, Wherry states that inductive preaching is an effective method for preaching funerals. He compares the inductive preacher to a docent in a museum taking listeners on a guided tour of biblical content. The preacher introduces the hearers to the sermon, but does not force them to view the exhibit. When done well, this method facilitates "Aha!" moments in which the hearers perceive some biblical insight that sheds light on the life of the deceased.[25]

Wherry identifies the following guidelines for inductive sermons:

1. They must be textual, always anchored in the biblical text to keep the focus on the message of biblical transformation.
2. They assist the hearers in drawing connections between the text and the story (typically some aspect of the life story of the deceased in funerals) using transitional phrases, word pictures, and/or quotations from songs.
3. They are amorphous in terms of structure, not likely to have three neat points of exposition and a poem at the end.[26]

A Eulogy: The Perfect Goodbye

I developed the eulogy "The Perfect Goodbye" for a patient who came on our hospice service in the final days of life. I completed an initial visit with the patient's spouse while the patient was in a coma-like state, receiving morphine for pain management. After the patient's death, I had one bereavement visit with the spouse to plan the funeral.

During initial visits, I want to understand the relationship that the spouse has with the patient. Typically, one of the first open-ended questions I ask couples is, "Tell me how you met. And, was it love at first sight?" These two questions allow the couple to start reflecting on the beginning of their relationship in contrast to experiencing the imminent end. Perhaps it's the magical, whimsical perception of the imagery of love at first sight, that invokes the common response of a smile or laugh followed by something funny like, "Oh, no. I couldn't stand him at first." Sometimes the answer is yes followed by a story about being set up on a blind date or seeing her across the room at a dance hall during the Second World War. Love at first sight inserts appropriate humor and a little levity within the conversation.

During the visitations, I listen for the character traits of the patient, aspects of life that are important to the family that may or may not include church and religion, and idiosyncrasies that are unique to the patient and family. I also listen for life stressors, perceived failures, and mistakes because often they can be landmines to avoid or areas to highlight as overcoming triumph. When I sit down to write the eulogy, I think through all of the limited information I have received in order to figure out the best imagery to highlight the life of the deceased.

In the specific example below, the spouse talked about meeting the patient during a time in her life when she was not looking for love. For her, it was love at first. She said, "I knew I loved him the moment I laid eyes on him." She talked about his beautiful hair and his pretty eyes. The important aspects of the patient's life expressed by the spouse was his world travels, vacationing with friends, being a military vet, and his close relationships with his coworkers. Unique to the patient was his love of the *Phantom of the Opera*, *Star Wars*, and peanut butter and jelly sandwiches. Due to the patient's Irish ancestry, they married on St. Patrick's Day.

Regarding religion, they were both divorcees with distinct childhood religious affiliations. She was United Methodist and he was Catholic. Neither attended church much as adults. Also, the patient felt rejected by the Catholic Church because he could no longer take communion after his divorce. To take communion again, the patient needed to formally annul his previous marriages. All of this information was expressed by the spouse during my pastoral and bereavement visitations.

Considering this information, I chose to develop the eulogy with the imagery of saying goodbye. Drawing on Jesus saying goodbye to his beloved friends at the communion table allows me to reclaim the patient's Christianity and his faith, which were very important to him. The version of the eulogy offered here is a modified version of what I actually delivered. In real life, during the end of the eulogy where I raise the chalice and bread in remembrance of Jesus, I actually replaced the chalice and bread with milk and a peanut butter and jelly sandwich. Milk and peanut butter and jelly was the patient's favorite meal. This replacement is not suitable for a practicing Catholic who believes in the Eucharist being the true body and blood of Christ. However, given the deceased's perceived rejection by the Catholic Church, this replacement further substantiated the deceased's life with that of the love of God.

The milk and the peanut butter and jelly sandwich as the elements for communion at the end of the eulogy makes this an inductive sermon with an element of surprise. The entire eulogy paints the picture of what a perfect goodbye looks like through an interpretive narrative of the ministry of Jesus. The suspense leads to the "Aha!" moment of actually saying "goodbye" through a ritual of remembrance of Communion.

Eulogy: The Perfect Goodbye[27]

The sermonic text, Luke 22:14–20, reads as follows:

When the hour came, he took his place at the table, and the apostles with him.

He said to them, "I have eagerly desired to eat this Passover
with you before I suffer.
for I tell you, I will not eat it until it is fulfilled in the
kingdom of God."
Then he took a cup, and after giving thanks and said, "Take
this and divide it among yourselves,
for I tell you that from now on I will not drink of the fruit
of the vine until the kingdom of God comes."
Then he took a loaf of bread, and when he had given thanks
he broke it and gave it to them, saying, "This is my
body, which is given for you. Do this in remembrance
of me."
And he did the same with the cup after supper, saying, "This
cup that is poured out for you is the new covenant in
my blood."

It's hard to say goodbye to those we love. And, is there such a thing as a GOOD-BYE when speaking to those we love dearly, persons that we would like to be with forever? Furthermore, as we leave our loved ones, I suspect there are more significant things we would say, rather than just goodbye, if we knew our time was drawing near.

In the text this afternoon, Jesus has the monumental task of saying goodbye to his beloved disciples. He knew the time had come for the fulfillment of scripture when he would be crucified on the cross. He gathered the disciples in the upper room to celebrate the Passover, as was customary during this period. But this time, the celebration was different. Unbeknownst to the disciples, this would be the Last Supper, the last Passover Celebration with Jesus here on earth, the last meal they would ever share with their companion and friend. But Jesus knew this was the Last Supper. He knew that this was his opportunity to say goodbye. Therefore, he sets a precedent for the perfect goodbye.

The first thing that Jesus shows us is that goodbyes are to celebrate life. In verse 15, Jesus says, "I have eagerly desired to eat this Passover with you before I suffer." It is no coincidence that Jesus plans the goodbye during the Passover meal. If we remember from the Old Testament, Passover comes the tenth plague where the Lord decided to kill the firstborn son in all of Egypt. You remember the story, Moses said to Pharaoh let my people go and the Lord hardened Pharaoh's heart. In order for the firstborn son to be spared, the Israelites placed the blood of the lamb on their doors, so that the death angel would *PASS OVER* their house. After the death of the first-born sons, Pharaoh relented and set the Israelites free. The Passover ritual not only celebrates the Israelites' freedom from slavery, but it also celebrates the lives that were spared, the firstborn sons.

So, as we say goodbye to Jason S. Williams, let us celebrate his life and all the things that make him uniquely Jason. The Lord gave him to us for 52 years, 3 months and 18 days. He lived a full life traveling the world, serving our country, enjoying the simple things in life—love and laughter. Teach us to number our days so that we, too, can live life to the fullest, loving and laughing freely.

As a retired military veteran, we can honestly say that the death angel passed over Jason in times of war as he served this country with distinction. Though we wish the death angel had passed over him once again, we can still celebrate his life by doing what Jesus did because a perfect goodbye is one that celebrates life by eating, drinking, and enjoying our family and friends.

The second thing that Jesus shows us is that goodbyes are to cherish love. We cherish love by telling our love stories. In verse 20, Jesus tells the love story of the gospel. He says, "This cup that is poured out for you is the new covenant in my blood." Here Jesus alludes to his blood being poured out on the cross on Calvary for the forgiveness of our sins. Is this not the ultimate love story, a story of unconditional, sacrificial love, representative of the covenant between us and our Savior? God so loved the world that he gave his only begotten son, that whosoever believes in him shall not perish, but have eternal life (John 3:16). That's love.

A perfect goodbye cherishes love by sharing our love stories. Share the story of a mother and father who fell in love with Jason the first time you laid eyes on him. Tell the story of the first time you held your beautiful son in your arms. Share the love story of a wife who wasn't looking for love, but love found her anyway. Tell the love story of co-workers who lovingly looked out for Jason at work during the onset of his illness. Share the love story of friends who vacationed with Jason. Share the love story of a family who fell in love with Kristen because they knew, the third time was the charm for Jason. Tell the love story that was built on the covenant that was made 13 years ago on St. Patrick's Day; for better or for worse, until death do us part. Tell the story of that unconditional, sacrificial love that loved Jason through the dark side of his illness all the way to eternal life. Tell the story because that's how we cherish our love.

The last thing that Jesus shows us about goodbyes is that a perfect goodbye continues the legacy. In verse 19 Jesus says, "This is my body, which is given for you. Do this in remembrance of me." We celebrate the Last Supper in remembrance of Christ's unconditional love for us through his crucifixion on the cross for the redemption of our sins. Continue the legacy of Christ through our unconditional love for one another on earth. Our love draws people to us, as the love of Christ draws us to the Lord. Share this love with one another freely. Do this in remembrance of Christ.

In remembrance of Jason, do rituals that honor his legacy. How are the grandchildren going to know of Jason's character prior to his illness, if we don't do rituals in remembrance of him? Go see the *Phantom of the Opera*, do this in remembrance of him. Watch the *Star Wars* movies, do this in remembrance of him. Eat a peanut butter and jelly sandwich, do this in remembrance of him. We will continue the legacy of Jason S. Williams by coming together as family and friends, eating, drinking, loving and laughing not only because Jason would want us to do this, but because that is the precedent set by Jesus Christ.

This Irish gal raises the chalice and a piece of bread and says: "Do this in remembrance of the life, death, burial and resurrection of Jesus Christ."[28] Because of Jason's water baptism into the Kingdom of God, today, we celebrate his life, cherish his love, and continue his legacy, believing in the promise of eternal life with our Lord and Savior Jesus Christ. We will be reunited with Jason and Jesus one day!" God bless you. Amen.

Eulogy Summary

The eulogy uses the sermonic scripture from Luke 22:14–20, The Last Supper. In the text, Jesus gathers his beloved disciples in the upper room to celebrate the Jewish holiday, the Passover. Passover comes the tenth plague, where the Lord decided to kill the firstborn sons in Egypt as a punishment to Pharaoh. Pharaoh would not heed the directives of God to release the Israelites from slavery in Egypt. Moses instructed the Israelites to kill a lamb and place the blood of the lamb on their doorpost. The death angel passed over the homes with the blood of the lamb, saving their first-born sons. Without the blood on the door, the death angel killed the first-born sons. After the plague, Pharaoh released the Israelites from captivity. Passover celebrates the Israelites' freedom from slavery and the lives that were spared during the pass over, the firstborn sons.

Jesus knew that the time had come for the fulfillment of scripture, when he would be crucified on the cross. Unbeknownst to the disciples, this would be the Last Supper, the last Passover Celebration with Jesus on earth. Since Jesus knew this was the Last Supper, in the sermon, I suggest that Jesus models the perfect goodbye by showing us how to say goodbye to our loved ones.

The relevant question, not explicitly identified in the sermon, is how do we experience the perfect goodbye? The moves of consciousness answer the relevant question. We experience the perfect goodbye when we: (1) celebrate the life of the "saint," (2) cherish the love of the "saint," and (3) continue the legacy of the "saint." Each move has a sub-move that provides further explanation. We celebrate life by sharing meals with family and friends. We cherish love by telling our love stories. We continue the legacy by doing activities in remembrance of our loved ones. Table 2 provides a summary of the eulogy as outlined in the preceding paragraphs.

Table 2: Eulogy Summary:

Sermonic Text	Luke 22:14–20
Sermon Title	The Perfect Goodbye
Sermonic Theme	Saying goodbye
Scripture Context	Passover Meal Celebration (The Last Supper)
Moves	The perfect goodbye celebrates life.
	The perfect goodbye cherishes love.
	The perfect goodbye continues the legacy.
Sub-moves	We celebrate life by sharing meals with friends and family.
	We cherish love by telling our love stories.
	We continue the legacy by doing activities in remembrance.

Eulogy Evaluation

The biblical text meets Henry Mitchell's elements of a meaningful experiential encounter with the word. The text has the following components: 1) a positive behavioral purpose that is explained in the text; and 2) the life application of the behavioral purpose is the primary focus of the eulogy. The behavioral purpose of saying goodbye to our loved ones is implicitly stated in the text when Jesus tells his beloved disciples in verses 15 and 16, "He said to them, "I have eagerly desired to eat this Passover with you before I suffer. For I tell you, I will not eat it until it is fulfilled in the kingdom of God." Jesus implies that he will not eat until the fulfillment of his destiny; crucifixion on the cross, burial in a tomb, and resurrection on the third day. With that understanding of the biblical text, the sermon focuses on the behavioral purpose of saying goodbye to our loved ones. Therefore, the title of the eulogy is "The Perfect Goodbye."

Jesus models the perfect goodbye while saying goodbye to his disciples. The life application of saying goodbye is relevant in the setting of a funeral, considering that funerals represent closure, finality of death, and as Thomas Long would say, the last mile of the journey. In light of the funeral, saying goodbye is a positive behavior. The manner in which Jesus says goodbye is positive too. The moves of consciousness draw directly from the Biblical text to explain how we, the mourners, express the perfect goodbye to our loved ones.

The eulogy includes the three elements that Mitchell claims are necessary for an experiential encounter of the word: vivid details; a vicarious experience; and homiletic moves in consciousness. Vivid details represent "the kinds of authentic, historical, fill-in details that make a person, place, thing, or a whole story come to life in the mental processes and total experience of the hearer."[29] The understanding of the Passover Meal as a celebration of freedom and life presents the crucial idea that develops the first move. The biblical text does not discuss the details of Passover. Therefore, I included the description of the historical pass over experience, which constitutes vivid details.

The context of the scripture imposed upon the milieu of the funeral creates a vicarious experience. While encountering the word, the hearers are experiencing saying goodbye to their loved one who died. Due to this connection, the hearers relate to Jesus. Since the audience can picture themselves in Jesus' situation, the moves examine Jesus' actions to exemplify the behavior for the hearers to emulate. The moves fulfill the task of describing known images that convey parallel meanings by explaining how Jesus expresses his goodbye to the disciples, modeling how the hearers can express goodbye to the deceased "saint."[30] Lastly, the sermon meets Mitchell's requirement of concluding with a final celebration of the text and its purpose. The purpose of the text is to say goodbye to our loved ones. In summary, Jesus held up the cup and bread, gave thanks, and told the disciples to drink and eat in remembrance of me. The sermon concludes with the preacher holding the deceased's favorite food, a peanut butter and jelly sandwich, saying "Here's to Jason S. Williams. We celebrate your life. We cherish your love. We continue your legacy." The ending actually says goodbye to the deceased "saint" using the moves of consciousness.

As shown in Table 3, the eulogy includes phrases representative of all eight purposes of a good funeral sermon. Also, the table describes how the eulogy fulfills the purpose and where the purpose is located within the three moves of consciousness.

Table 3: Eulogy Evaluation – Eight Purposes of a Good Funeral Sermon

Purposes of a Good Funeral Sermon	Purpose Included? Yes/No	Evidence in the Eulogy	Location
Kerygmatic	Yes	The love story of the gospel message. John 3:16	Move #2
Oblational	Yes	The use of specific examples of our love stories.	Move #2
Ecclesial	Yes	Celebrate life through fellowship with family and friends.	Move #1
Therapeutic	Yes	Believing in the promises of God, eternal life with Christ.	Move #3
Eucharistic	Yes	Be thankful for God's blessings and share those stories.	Move #3
Missional	Yes	Continue the legacy of Christ by loving one another.	Move #3
Commemorative	Yes	Continue the legacy by doing things in remembrance.	Move #3
Educational	Yes	Teach us to number our days to live life to the fullest.	Move #1

"The Perfect Goodbye" as an Act of Prophetic Proclamation

The eulogy entitled "The Perfect Goodbye" is an act of prophetic proclamation because it gives voice to the Christian witness of a marginalized group, persons who identify as Christian and live outside of the Christian religious community. Jason, the deceased, was a twice divorced Catholic who married Kristen as his third wife. Due to his divorce and remarriage, he was no longer in good standing with the Catholic Church. Since Jason did not vow a marriage of chastity, he was unable to partake in the Eucharist sacrament. Jason was not active in any religious community of faith. Jason's spouse, Kristen grew up in Methodist churches. However, as an adult she did not have any church affiliation either. Jason and Kristen considered themselves Christian and believed that their lives reflected values representative of a Christian faith.

As an act of prophetic proclamation, "The Perfect Goodbye" welcomes these marginalized Christians as well as those within the gathered community into the sacred space to exemplify Jason's faith, honor his God, and comfort his loved one's grieving hearts. The eulogy redeems Jason's value as a Christian by highlighting his Christian witness which is the lasting legacy that he leaves for those to cherish on earth. As a representative of the religious community of faith, I extended God's grace and mercy to Jason and welcomed him into the community.

CHAPTER **THREE**:

OUTCOMES AND MEANS OF EVALUATION

Having preached, read, and listened to many eulogies written for strangers or near-strangers, I grew curious about how other preachers approached this challenging phenomenon. Therefore, I interviewed clergy with experience preaching funerals for people they do not know. I talked to hospice chaplains, military chaplains, congregational pastors, and associate ministers to understand how each minister develops these particular types of sermons. Table 4 displays the characteristics of the ten clergy.

Table 4. Clergy Characteristics

#	Gender	Race	Current Ministerial Position	Denomination	Funeral Experience
1	Male	Black	Pastor	Baptist	Pastor
2	Female	Black	Hospital Chaplain (Resident)	African Methodist Episcopal	Pastor

3	Female	Black	Pastor	Disciples of Christ	Pastor
4	Female	Black	Associate Minister	Baptist	Associate Minister
5	Male	Black	Pastor	Baptist	On-call funeral clergy/ Associate Pastor/ Pastor
6	Male	Black	Hospice Chaplain	Baptist	Navy Chaplain
7	Male	Black	Pastor	Baptist	Pastor
8	Male	White	Pastor/ Hospice Chaplain	Lutheran	Pastor/ Hospice Chaplain
9	Male	Black	Minister for Seniors	International Council of Community Churches	Navy Chaplain
10	Female	Black	Air Force Chaplain	Baptist	Air Force Chaplain

The interviews consisted of the following questions:

1. What is the context in which you preached funeral sermons or eulogies?
2. Why were you asked/assigned to preach the funeral?
3. What was the goal of the funeral sermon or eulogy? (Maybe explicit or implicit) Examples include, unity in the community, comfort the bereaved family, salvation of those unsaved, etc.
4. Would you consider the sermon a funeral sermon or a eulogy? Why?
5. How do you prepare for the funeral sermon/eulogy?
6. How do you select the scripture? Any common scriptures used?

7. Do you use themes or topical funeral sermons? If so, what are the common ones?
8. If the person was Christian, did you address the deceased's Christian faith in the sermon? If so, how?
9. Were there any theological concepts that informed the sermon, such as heaven/hell, sin, good vs. evil, etc.? If so, how?
10. Do you have an invitation to discipleship (open the doors of the church)? Why or why not? If so, how?

Outcomes

Table 5. Summary of the Clergy's Answers

#	Eulogy or Funeral Sermon?	Meet with Family Yes or No?	Familiar Scripture Yes or No?	Themes Yes or No?	Christian faith addres-sed Yes or No?	Theo-logical Concepts: i.e., heaven/ hell Yes or No?	Altar Call Yes or No?
1	Eulogy	Y	N	N	Y	N	N
2	Eulogy	Y	N	N	Y	N	N
3	Funeral Sermon	Y	Y	N	Y	Rarely	At the family's request
4	Eulogy	Y	Y	N	N	N	At the family's request
5	Eulogy	Y	Y	Y	Y	Y	Y
6	Hybrid	Y	N	Y	Y	N	N
7	Eulogy	Y	N	Y	Y	N	At the family's request
8	Sem-antics	Y	N	N	Y	N	N

9	Eulogy	Y	Y	Y	Y	N	N
10	Eulogy	Y	N	Y	Y	N	N

From my interviews, I learned that preaching funerals for someone unknown to clergy is common. Whether in pastoral ministry or chaplaincy, many clergy preach funerals for people unknown to them. Several pastors mentioned that a couple of people died within the first month of their pastorate. Therefore, they had to preach funerals for long-time members who they did not know personally. One pastor said that she attended a funeral of one of her parishioner's mothers and upon arrival was notified that they did not have clergy designated to officiate nor give the eulogy. She talked to her parishioner and quickly pulled together a sermon.

The military chaplains surveyed preached funerals for people who were assigned to their unit, but not active in the spiritual life of the community. Hospice chaplains preached funerals for their deceased patients who they may have only visited once prior to their death. Even though this is a common occurrence, the method of preaching a funeral for someone unknown is trial by fire.

Funeral Sermon vs. Eulogy

My interviewees, despite coming from different generations and ministerial contexts, prefer eulogies to funeral sermons. Even those who preach funeral sermons attempt to find ways in which they can personalize the sermon. One pastor said that the personalization of the funeral sermon gives the deceased dignity even in death. Another pastor said that he may not have known them, but somebody knew them; that's the reason he attempts to personalize the message. A hospice chaplain mentioned that the difference between a funeral sermon and a eulogy are mere semantics. He preaches a personalized

Gospel message that references the deceased in a meaningful way. The common thread amongst all clergy I interviewed is that they want to personalize the Gospel message in light of the life of the deceased in order to honor the deceased and encourage the hearers. To do so, all of them attempt to meet with the deceased's family and friends.

Length of the Funeral Sermon or Eulogy

More experienced clergy said they preach ten to fifteen-minute sermons for funerals. One pastor said, "It's not about me. I say what I need to say and sit down." Other clergy stated that they preach twenty-five to thirty-minute eulogies, as if it were Sunday morning. Yet one pastor said it depends on the context of the funeral. According to him, a twenty-five-minute eulogy is the expectation of a Homegoing Celebration in his Black Baptist church tradition. When preaching funerals for other faith traditions, this pastor tailors his sermon to a motivational style message and limits the length to fifteen minutes.

Familiar Scripture

The question asking about familiar scripture refers to the use of scriptures as sermonic text, such as Psalm 23, Psalm 27, John 3:16, John 14:2, and other scripture that people "generally" have heard regardless of their church affiliation or lack thereof. Some clergy stayed away from familiar scripture for a variety of reasons. A few said they did not want to appear generic or phony. Others preferred to tailor the scripture based on the conversations about the deceased's life. Many clergy use the deceased's favorite scripture as sermonic text if it is mentioned during conversations with the family. Often the deceased's favorite scripture is something characterized as familiar, such as the twenty-third Psalm. One pastor said that he tries to understand why a particular verse was the deceased's favorite and then preaches from that perspective.

When asked about sermonic text, several clergy mentioned books that they reference when choosing scripture. The three resources are summarized below:

1. *Minister's Manual for Funerals* by Al Cadenhead, Jr. – The author gives advice on funeral preparations from the moment clergy hears about the death through pastoral support for bereavement follow up. For example, some advice on funeral logistics is to deliver the message at the head of the casket. More pastoral advice is to write down the date of the death, so that clergy can visit the family on the first anniversary. This book also includes sample sermons for clergy to use during the funeral service.
2. *A Trumpet in Darkness: Preaching to Mourners* by Robert G. Hughes – The author correlates scripture with particular deaths, such as suicide and the death of a child. He also provides sample sermons and helpful insights on funeral preparation, such as the importance of reframing mourners' images with images of hope.
3. *Minister's Service Book: For Pulpit and Parish* by Jesse Jai McNeil – Specifically for funerals, this book has a chapter entitled "The Burial of the Dead." The author provides prayers, appropriate passages from scripture, and other assistance for funerals of both Christians and non-Christians from a National Baptist perspective.

The majority of clergy interviewed determine scripture based on the following characteristics: how the person died, the deceased's particular age, or how they lived their life. One pastor mentioned the following sermonic text used for specific situations:

- Job 1:21 – for children
- John 3:1-6 – for older people

- Hebrews 11:5-6 – for people who walked with the Lord for a long time
- Proverbs 31 – for Godly women
- 2 Timothy 4:6-8 – for people who battled illness, such as cancer

Several clergy use familiar scripture for readings in the liturgy. For example, in some Baptist funeral traditions, there is an Old Testament and a New Testament reading, which may include Psalm 23 and John 14:2. Other traditions may use the Apostle's Creed or the Lord's Prayer as the familiar reference. Two clergy had similar understandings of the reason for using familiar scripture in the funeral service. One chaplain said that familiar scripture is like coming down the stairs in the dark. If you're having trouble finding the next step, familiarity during the grieving period is like the hand rail that leads you down the stairs safely. Another chaplain expressed that familiarity with scriptures and symbols provides comfort in times of grief. Therefore, he uses familiar scripture for sermonic text and wears a clergy collar for funerals.

Themes

The question on themes refers to the use of broad topics such as love or laughter, etc. Some clergy said that topical preaching is not their traditional form of preaching and they do not change their homiletic methodology for a funeral. One pastor said that she preaches topically when she "really" does not know the person. For example, if the only information she receives about the deceased is that he loved music, then she will preach a funeral sermon on the joy of music. Generally speaking, one pastor preaches on death, resurrection, and life after death as her major themes during the funeral sermon of someone unknown to her. Lastly, one chaplain said that she focuses on the theme of leaving a legacy in most of her eulogies.

Christian Faith

Most clergy attempt to address the deceased's Christian faith, if that information is discussed while meeting with the family. However, the deceased's faith is not necessarily a primary topic of conversation for clergy. The reality is that in most situations the clergy does not know the deceased because of their lack of church affiliation. Typically, the lack of church affiliation corresponds to the lack of the hallmarks of faith; being a prayer warrior, having a church title, giving generously of one's time, talents, and treasures to the church. Therefore, clergy attempt to extrapolate Christian values, like love from the deceased's life. One pastor received these words of wisdom from his father in the ministry, "If you can't talk about anything else, talk about two things: the person's relationship with God and their relationship with others."

Instead of focusing on the deceased's Christian faith, many clergy mentioned the importance of preaching an authentic message grounded in a Biblical passage that reflects the life of the deceased. For example, one chaplain described a situation where she was asked to preach a funeral for a young man who she did not know well. When talking to the man's mother, she spoke of a good boy who exemplified love in so many Christian ways. The chaplain asked to speak to the young man's girlfriend and other friends. They painted a different picture by describing a man who loved casinos, Black Jack, and the "fast life." To be authentic to the deceased and not shame the mother, the chaplain preached a celebratory message of having family cookouts in the backyard, playing spades, and having fun. According to the chaplain, preaching an authentic message created a sacred space for all to celebrate the life of the deceased, even his friends outside of the religious Christian community.

Theological Concepts

Several clergy mentioned theodicy, "defense of God's goodness and omnipotence in view of the existence of evil," as the theological concept they regularly highlight in funerals for people unknown to them.[1] When dealing with grief, reflecting on theodicy is a way to comfort the gathered community prophetically by naming evils and reframing life based on the spiritual perspective of God. Most clergy refrained from preaching about heaven or hell. One chaplain said that the funeral is not the time to scare people into religion by preaching on hell. The one clergy who preaches about heaven or hell does so as a reminder that heaven and hell are real. This same clergy is the only person interviewed who always includes some type of invitation to discipleship in his funeral sermons.

Invitation to Discipleship

Of all the funerals I have attended while researching for this book, I only experienced one funeral with an invitation to discipleship. As I sat in the pew, I was shocked that the clergy was asking people to walk down the aisle and give their life to Christ. To me, this was a manipulative act that preyed on the power of grief. This experience was foreign to me. I admit that my reaction may not have been so negative if the invitation to discipleship had been customary in my experience of funerals. I recognize that some faith traditions may include an invitation to discipleship within their funeral liturgy. Some clergy believe it is their professional obligation to conclude with an invitation to discipleship that offers salvation to unbelievers and an opportunity to wayward persons to rededicate their lives to Christ.

Even though my experience of the altar call was negative, in another instance, I was surprised that the preacher did not include an altar call. I attended a funeral in which the preacher repeatedly talked about making a decision to follow Christ, but never gave anyone the opportunity to make the confession of faith to the Lord. Since it was heavily discussed in the pulpit, I expected the pastor to say, "If that is your decision today, meet me after the service or bow your head and repeat the sinner's prayer with me." There are ways to conduct the invitation to discipleship without asking the gathered community to walk down the aisle in front of the casket during the funeral service.

The pastor I interviewed who always includes an invitation to discipleship does so because he believes it is an important part of his Black Baptist tradition, even in the funeral worship experience. Typically, he does not ask people to walk down the aisle. He asks the gathered community to close their eyes and bow their heads to repeat the sinner's prayer. However, most clergy stated that they do not invite mourners to discipleship because the funeral is not the time for evangelism. One pastor thought the invitation to discipleship inappropriately takes the focus away from the deceased and shifts it towards whoever is accepting or rededicating their life to Christ. Several clergy said they had experienced funerals with altar calls and felt as if this manipulated the grieving gathered community. One pastor believed that the invitation to discipleship during a funeral is emotionally driven and not a decision made soberly and of a sound mind. Another pastor mentioned that in his experience, people get caught up in the moment and accept Christ. They said that when the person talks to the deacon after the funeral, they generally have a change of heart and ask the deacon to just pray for them. The pastors who occasionally invite mourners to discipleship said that they only do so at the family's request. Sometimes the saved family knows that unsaved persons will be attending the funeral. Therefore, they want an invitation to discipleship to give the unsaved persons an opportunity to accept Christ.

Pastoral Care for Preaching Funerals for People Unknown to Clergy

From the interviews, clergy meet the closest relatives of the deceased; a spouse, children, parents, friends, and even co-workers (military unit) in order to preach a eulogy or personalized funeral sermon of someone they do not know well. It is a best practice to meet with more than one person in order to get a more well-rounded perspective of the deceased. Several chaplains meet the family at a place that is special to the deceased, such as the deceased's home, so they can observe pictures on the walls, personal items on the shelves, and books that reflect the deceased's hobbies. One chaplain discussed how he sits in the deceased's favorite chair to see what they saw each day. He described himself as a "sensor" needing to get a feel for the deceased. Is there a Bible next to the deceased's favorite chair? Is it worn? What's the decor of the kitchen? Is it a place that ushered in the spirit of hospitality? Are there plants signifying a nurturer? These are the types of questions the chaplain asks himself as he observes the living area.

Additionally, while meeting with family, clergy should ask open-ended questions or statements to get to know the deceased, such as: what is your fondest memory of John and tell me about John? When considering the personalized funeral sermon or eulogy, some clergy ask the family, "Is there something specific you want me to say?" Often, the family has something extremely special that they want conveyed in the service. For example, I preached at a funeral for a British woman who I met once prior to her death on our hospice service. When I talked to the woman's daughter during the bereavement visit, she wanted me to say that her mother was an All-American gal. Through listening to the daughter's stories, I learned that this British woman became an All-American gal by living the American Dream of being a successful entrepreneur. I expressed these sentiments in the words of reflection.

One of the best practices specific to those with military chaplaincy experience is pastoral follow-up. The military chaplains intentionally set themselves up for continued pastoral support during their bereavement visits. Follow-up is not mandatory, but is frequently needed due to the stress of deployment and the pervasiveness of suicide. One military chaplain said that it is his responsibility to ensure that the unit processes their grief and maintains mission readiness, which is why he focuses on continued pastoral support. Another military chaplain experienced a high number of suicides which caused her to be more proactive with pastoral support in hopes of preventing further deaths by suicide. Regardless of the reason for continued pastoral support, bereavement follow-up is a best practice approach for funerals of people unknown to the clergy.

Bereavement support is an appropriate time to meet the needs of the community through evangelism. Evangelism is continuing the relationship that was initiated during the funeral. Make follow-up phone calls to assess their bereavement needs, not only at the one-year anniversary, but periodically throughout the entire year: one month, three months, six months, and nine months after the death of their loved one. If clergy are ministers of a church that offers grief support groups, invite the bereaved to join a group. At some point along their grieving process, invite the bereaved family to worship services.

In summary, there are many perspectives on preaching funerals for people unknown to clergy. All of the clergy I interviewed attempt to honor the life of the deceased in their funeral sermon or eulogy. These interviews validated my own perspective of preaching a eulogy that honors the life of the deceased and identifies their Christian witness as a legacy remaining for the gathered community. Even though the deceased may not present a Christian witness that reflects the hallmarks of traditional Christianity, I and other clergy seek to preach an authentic message that extrapolates Christian values from the deceased's life.

CHAPTER **FOUR**:

HOMILETIC METHODS FOR PREACHING FUNERALS FOR PEOPLE UNKNOWN TO THE CLERGY

Drawing on the interviews and on my own experience preaching funerals for people I do not know, I believe that there are three methods that can help clergy honor the life of the deceased by sharing the Gospel message and comforting the gathered community. The three methods are studying the obituary, preaching on a theme, and finding contextual similarities. In the following, I briefly discuss the meaning of each method, and for the latter two, I offer eulogies that illustrate their application.

Studying the Obituary

Often, the obituary gives the clergy a detailed look into the deceased's life. By studying the obituary, clergy can extrapolate key characteristics of the deceased to inform a broader talking point in the eulogy. For example, if the obituary says that Larry was a dedicated member of the Masons and was married to his wife, Mary, for over forty years, clergy speak on broader notions of commitment and being family oriented. Commitment is evidenced by Larry's dedicated membership in the Masons and being a family man captures his marriage of forty years. Even though in most funerals the gathered community silently reads the obituary, this approach works during the preaching moment because the gathered community is not hearing the same words that they just read in the obituary.

Preaching on a Theme

Two of the most common themes for preaching a funeral are saying goodbye and leaving a legacy. When I preach these themes, I use the family's stories to paint a picture of how to say goodbye based on the life of the deceased and how we should live to honor the legacy of the deceased. The following themed eulogy is an example of a prophetic eulogy I preached for a hospice patient. Initially, the patient declined chaplain services. Then he wanted to be baptized, so I visited him to make sure he understood the baptismal sacrament. I baptized him and several family members. After the baptism, I spoke with the patient on the phone a couple of times, but he did not accept any more chaplaincy visits. I completed a bereavement visit with the deceased's stepdaughter.

The theme of the eulogy is leaving a lasting legacy. The sermonic text, John 13:34–35, reads as follows:

> "I give you a new commandment, that you love one another.
> Just as I have loved you, you also should love one another.
> By this everyone will know that you are my disciples, if you have love for one another."

Eulogy: Leaving a Lasting Legacy

Often, I hear men say that if they have any children, they really want a boy in order to carry on the family name; a son represents their legacy, ensuring that the bloodline continues. Typically, these men are excited about having a beautiful, healthy girl, but their heart's desire is to have a son to continue the legacy of their surname. Because we know that women, especially in the South, normally drop their maiden names and take the last name of their husbands once they say "I do." And typically (not always), the children take the last name of their father.

David Hill had two biological daughters and one step-daughter, but since he didn't believe in step, we'll say he had three daughters. Even though he did not have a son, I submit to you today that David left a lasting legacy; a legacy that we will cherish forever; a legacy that will continue for generations to come; a legacy that did not pass away upon his death, but shines forth even more brightly than ever before. David Lamont Hill left a lasting legacy of love.

Jesus describes this legacy of love in the text this morning as he teaches us about his new commandment. In John 13:34–35 Jesus says, "I give you a new commandment, that you love one another. Just as I have loved you, you also should love one another. By this everyone will know that you are my disciples, if you have love for one another."

Jesus is simply saying that you will know my disciples by their love for others. The love that Jesus gives will flow through the disciple, which will then be shown to others. David showed the love of Christ to his friends and family. This lasting legacy of love is the essence of David Lamont Hill. This text highlights who he is at his core—a man who never met a stranger; a man who talked to all of his neighbors; a man who was always helpful and willing to give of himself for someone else.

Yesterday as I sat with Michelle, she shared a story about how she ran into an old friend from the neighborhood. This friend gave her condolences for the passing of Paw Paw. As many of you know, Paw

Paw was David's nickname to all the neighborhood kids. Then, the friend asked Michelle, what was his name? You mean to tell me after all these years; you let your child get to know David and even mentor your child as the neighborhood Paw Paw and you don't even know his name? I told Michelle that's the beauty of Mr. Hill's life. They may not have known his name, but they knew his nickname. Nicknames are personal. When you call someone by their nickname, typically, you've known them for a long time. Nicknames signify a special relationship, a personal friendship, a bond between people. Often times, nicknames are terms of endearment reflecting a loving relationship. David's name wasn't important. They did not know his name, but they knew his love. David's love for the neighborhood kids, their families, and friends is the lasting legacy that he leaves with us this day.

This morning, I want to help us understand this lasting legacy of love because it's much easier said than done. To love others, you must first love yourself. Love who you are and the person that God created you to be. This isn't a narcissist, taking selfies in the bathroom, posting your every move on Twitter kind of love. This is a mature love that comes from; accepting who you are, the good, the bad, and the ugly, acknowledging your faults, working on those growing edges, learning from your mistakes, and celebrating your accomplishments. To love yourself is to take responsibility for your actions and to be accountable to the people in your life who you say you love.

Now, I don't know what happened in Mr. Hill's earlier days, growing up in the country, being a young father, and a military veteran who fought in the Vietnam War. But one thing I do know is that the events in his life shaped him to be an honorable man of great character with a loving heart. David was not perfect, I'm sure he had many regrets in life. But he used life as a great teacher and learned from his mistakes. Someone who loves themselves is able to forgive themselves for their mistakes and move on in life, recognizing that since they know better, they WILL do better. David did better for himself and the people around him. So, if we are to leave a lasting legacy like David, we must learn to love ourselves.

The last and most important thing we need to understand is that in order to leave a lasting legacy of love, we must have a relationship with Christ. Now, I didn't say you must go to church. As a preacher, I want you to find a church where you can grow and mature in your spiritual walk. The legacy of love is not about church; it's about building a relationship with Christ. David would tell you, "I'm no Bible thumper, but I love the Lord." In the final months of his life, David recognized that he had never been baptized. He wanted the peace of knowing that he was right with the Lord, covered by the blood of Jesus. I had the honor of baptizing him one Saturday morning.

In that baptismal pool, David Lamont Hill rededicated his life to Christ and gave his grandsons the best gift that any Paw Paw can give. He led his grandsons towards a relationship with Christ by receiving the gift of salvation. The grandsons wanted to be baptized because their Paw Paw was being baptized, so he had discussions with them about the significance of baptism and a relationship with Christ.

The first step in having this relationship is the confession of faith. The word of God tells us in Romans 10:9 that if we confess with our mouths the Lord Jesus, and believe in our heart that God raised him from the dead, then we shall be saved. Salvation is free. But discipleship will cost you. Loving others is a discipleship issue, following that which God has commanded us to do. When we love like God commands us to love, it means giving up the very best that we have to offer, making a sacrifice for those we love. If we are to love others, it means we must sacrifice some things. Love is sacrificial. I'm sure there were many times that David had to sacrifice himself for his family and friends, giving up something that was near and dear to him for the needs of his friends, Michelle or the grandkids.

Let me see if I can make it plain. I can remember when I was in high school and I was at a baseball game with some friends. I had a pack of Starburst. One of my friend's little brother asked me for a Starburst. I gave him a yellow one. I don't really like yellow. I like red, so giving up the yellow didn't cost me anything. The boy's mother then asked me for a Starburst. I gave her a yellow one too. Then she looked at me and said, "Hmmm... you must not like yellow." Now, today if I had a pack of Starburst and someone asked me for one, I would give them a red Starburst because I understand this concept of sacrificial love. I'm willing to give up the very best I have. I'm willing to sacrifice myself in order to fulfill your needs.

This understanding of loving others shown as sacrificing your very best comes from the love of the Almighty God. John 3:16 says, "For God so loved the world that he gave his only Son, so that everyone who believes in him may not perish but may have eternal life." Late on Friday evening, this loving God looked down on our beloved "David." He said Paw Paw; you've done all that you can do. Now it's time for you to stand. Stand on my word. Stand on my promises. In John 14:2, Jesus Christ said, "In my Father's house there are many dwelling places. If it were not so, would I have told you that I go to prepare a place for you?" Early on Friday morning, the Lord said, "David, your mansion is ready." It's time for you to come meet your maker.

Deliverance came for "David." No more chains holding you. You're free "David," free from the jail of your frail and fragile body. No more sickness. No more sorrow. No more headaches. No more heartache. You've done all that was required of you. You followed my new commandment to love each other just as I have loved you. Beloved you are my disciple and now it's time for you to receive your crown of glory. David, they might not know your name, but the Lord knows your name! You can hear the Lord say, "Well done, my good and faithful servant. Well done." Amen.

Leaving a Lasting Legacy as an Act of Prophetic Proclamation

This eulogy is an act of prophetic proclamation because it gives voice to the Christian witness of a marginalized group, persons who identify as Christian and live outside of the Christian religious community. David, the deceased, was raised in a country Baptist church in the South. He could not remember being baptized as a child. As he was approaching death, David wanted to ensure his salvation through the sacrament of baptism. Throughout David's life, he would tell people that he is no Bible thumper. Several people, including myself, mentioned this during David's funeral service. David did not have any church affiliation nor did he attend church regularly. Due to David's lack of traditional, Christian witness with regards to reading the Bible, attending church, and even being baptized, David viewed himself as a "less than" Christian, evident by his qualifiers, "I ain't no Bible thumper." However, David considered himself a Christian.

As an act of prophetic proclamation, "Leaving a Lasting Legacy" welcomes this marginalized Christian as well as those within the gathered community into the sacred space to exemplify David's faith, honor his God, and comfort his loved one's grieving hearts. The eulogy redeems David's value as a Christian by highlighting his Christian witness, which is the lasting legacy that he leaves for those to cherish on earth. As a representative of the religious community of faith, I extended God's grace and mercy to David and welcomed him into the community.

Contextual Similarities

Clergy can find Biblical contexts that are similar to the context in which the deceased died or the way in which the deceased lived. For example, as a hospice chaplain, I often meet people on their death bed.

When asked to preach the funeral, particularly for women, I use the sermonic text from Acts 9:36–42 where the disciple, Tabitha is sick and dying. Below is an example of a eulogy I preached for someone I did not know using the contextual similarities approach. Acts 9:36–42 reads as follows:

> Now in Joppa there was a disciple whose name was Tabitha, which in Greek is Dorcas. She was devoted to good works and acts of charity.
> At that time she became ill and died. When they had washed her, they laid her in a room upstairs.
> Since Lydda was near Joppa, the disciples, who heard that Peter was there, sent two men to him with the request, "Please come to us without delay."
> So Peter got up and went with them, and when he arrived, they took him to the room upstairs. All the widows stood beside him, weeping and showing tunics and other clothing that Dorcas had made while she was with them.
> Peter put all of them outside, and then he knelt down and prayed. He turned to the body and said, "Tabitha, get up." Then she opened her eyes, and seeing Peter, she sat up.
> He gave her his hand and helped her up. Then calling the saints and widows, he showed her to be alive.
> This became known throughout Joppa, and many believed in the Lord.

Eulogy with Contextual Similarities

The family asked me to speak this afternoon and as I was thinking about what to say, I could not help but to draw some comparisons of a scripture with a woman by the name of Tabitha and that of my experience with Mrs. Barry in her final hours. The scripture is taken from the book of Acts 9:36–42. In verse 36, we meet a woman by the name of Tabitha who was always doing good and helping the poor. She lived in the town of Joppa. In Joppa, Tabitha became sick and died. Her body was washed and placed in an upstairs room.

I had the distinct pleasure of meeting Mrs. Barry as she too was lying in a bed, sick and about to die. The nurse had come a little earlier and told the family not to move Mrs. Barry, to just let her be. As I was talking to the family, they began to share stories of her being prim and proper. The family didn't want her to come back and haunt them for not cleaning her up properly during her final hours. In order for Mrs. Barry to die with dignity, Ms. Grow and others began to wash her body and position her comfortably in the bed with grace.

Verse 37 tells us that Tabitha was placed in an upper room. In scripture, the power of God is revealed to us in upper rooms. The disciples shared the Last Supper with Jesus in the upper room. The prophet, Elisha, resurrected the Shunamites son in an upper room. The upper room is not special in of itself. The upper room was special because it was set apart by God, as a consecrated place, holy ground where we can experience the Glory of the Lord. That bedroom in which Mrs. Barry took her final breath is in fact an upper room, a holy place where we experienced God's glory, the miracle of death, the transition to eternal life.

After placing Tabitha in the upper room, the disciples sent two men to get Peter. In verse 38, the men urged Peter to come to Joppa to see about Tabitha. Upon Peter's arrival in Joppa, he went to the upper room where they had placed the woman's dead body. The widows stood around crying, mourning their loss, and showing Peter all of the robes and other clothes Tabitha had made them.

The significance of the widows was the fact that they tell us what kind of woman Tabitha was. She was a caring woman that valued everyone, even the least of these in society; those persons society disregarded and snubbed their nose at. In those days, most women didn't work for money. They didn't own property. Women stayed in their father's house until they got married, then the women were their husband's responsibility. A widow was a second-class citizen, society's problem, living on the generosity of others. Tabitha helped the widows.

As a retired waitress, could you imagine all of those persons that Mrs. Barry helped over the years, all of those who experienced the grace of God through her spirit of hospitality that welcomed them to the table? Can you see them mourning, like the widows, in that consecrated room, telling stories of their fond memories of Mrs. Barry? She had the opportunity to bless whosoever sat at her tables, to allow them to experience the love of God through her service.

Finally, in verse 40, Peter got down on his knees and prayed. He turned to the dead woman and said, "Tabitha, get up." She opened her eyes and sat up. Peter took Tabitha by the hand and helped her to her feet. Then he presented Tabitha alive to the believers, especially, the widows, those she helped.

As I sat with the family, they shared that Mrs. Barry was calling out the names of loved ones that had passed away. God allows our loved ones to come and usher us into eternity, those of us who are destined for Glory. For Mrs. Barry, it was not Peter that was called to come see about her. It was none other than the Lord. Early on Friday morning, the Lord said, "Rosa, get up! Rosa, get up!" Mrs. Barry opened her eyes and saw the Lord, along with her husband, and other loved ones that preceded her in death. Now God presents her to us as she experiences eternal life, alive and well in Glory.

Contextual Similarities Eulogy as an Act of Prophetic Proclamation

Like the previous example, this eulogy gives voice to persons who identify as Christian and live outside of the Christian religious community. Mrs. Barry, the deceased, was a devout Christian who remained active in African Methodist Episcopal (AME) church prior to her declining health. When she could no longer live independently, she moved down South with her granddaughter, Ms. Grow. For many years, Mrs. Barry was unable to attend church; therefore, she did not have any current church affiliation and lived outside of the Christian religious community. Like many elderly parishioners who are no longer able to attend church due to their declining health, Mrs. Barry represents a marginalized group that the universal church forgets sometimes. After a while, the home visits of Communion cease and the church bulletin stops coming in the mail along with the recording of Sunday worship services. On the other hand, the church may no longer receive Mrs. Barry's tithes and offerings.

Like David's eulogy, this eulogy is an act of prophetic proclamation that welcomes this marginalized Christian into the sacred worship to exemplify Mrs. Barry's faith, honor her God, and comfort her loved one's grieving hearts. One of the lasting legacies that Mrs. Barry leaves is the beautiful, loving relationship between her and her granddaughter. This relationship was evident by the sacred, ceremonial washing of Mrs. Barry's body towards the end of life. Based on Mrs. Barry's estranged relationship with the church towards the end of life, this eulogy redeems her value as a Christian by highlighting her Christian witness. As a representative of the religious community of faith, I extended God's grace and mercy to Mrs. Barry and welcomed her into the community.

CHAPTER **FIVE**:

CONCLUSION

During this research, I attended funeral services, researched historical funeral sermons, interviewed clergy, and preached eulogies for my hospice patients. I attended 102 funerals for my hospice patients and gave the words of comfort in the form of a sermon for 10 of those services. For the funerals that I attended, I had the opportunity to hear how other clergy deliver funeral sermons and eulogies. I collected several great sermon illustrations such as the imagery of running your fingers along the names of the war memorial. Also, I attended funeral services of other denominations. I found the Catholic liturgy to be the most riveting with their use of symbols and traditional burial protocols; ushering the priest and family into the sanctuary immediately behind the casket, placing the white pall over the casket symbolizing the white clothes worn during baptism, and sprinkling Holy Water onto the casket as a reminder of the deceased's baptism. During one Catholic funeral all believers were able to partake in Communion, whereas in most other Catholic funerals only Catholics received Communion. I found that I appreciate symbolism and other reminders of our faith traditions in funeral worship.

The interviews of other clergy had the greatest impact on my ministry towards the funerals of people I do not know well. Prior to the interviews, I never considered giving the bereaved family a copy of the sermon. One chaplain said that he always provides the family with a video of the sermon or the sermon manuscript. He believes that people don't remember what you said during the funeral, but they remember how you made them feel. A copy of the sermon allows them to hear what was said as they continue to process their grief by moving towards periods of reflection to heal their heartbreak.

On the one hand, I like the idea of giving a copy of the sermon to the bereaved family. This is a great keepsake similar to the funeral program. On the other hand, I'm not sure if remembering what was said during the funeral is all that important. There is a possibility that the video or manuscript could hinder the grieving process by allowing people to replay the funeral over and over again. I worry this could cause the bereaved to become "stuck." But I continue to consider this practice for future funerals.

Additionally, prior to the interviews, I never reflected on the use of familiar scripture. Generally speaking, I do not use familiar scripture as sermonic text, but I use familiar scripture during the liturgy of the Old Testament and New Testament readings. I agree with the two chaplains' perspective of familiarity as comfort during the time of grief. Based on their perspectives, which also align with Brad Braxton's writings, I now often consider incorporating familiar scripture and symbols during funeral worship.

Due to my own negative experience of the invitation to discipleship at a funeral, I never planned an invitation at a funeral in which I preached the sermon. However, after talking to other clergy, I would be more compelled to have an invitation to discipleship at the request of the family. Prior to the interviews, I believe I would have told the family no, if the situation arose. After some thought, I realize that the funeral is not about me. It's about the family and making the bereaved feel comforted during their time of grief. Now, if the family requests an invitation to discipleship, I would lean towards a modified version without having people walk down the aisle.

In my initial inquiries to clergy with experience preaching funerals for people they do not know, I realized that context plays a role in the point of departure for their funeral sermons. For example, a congregational pastor officiated the funeral for a diaconate member's son who was murdered. The son was an inactive member of the church and relatively unknown to her. The pastor used the book of Job to talk about life's tragedies that do not make sense. Her pastoral message focused on comforting the family.

In the death of this young man, the circumstances involved alcohol and were less than desirable. His death had cultural undertones of communal shame and judgment, as some believed that the deceased should not have been at the location where he was murdered. The pastor's funeral sermon addressed the self-righteous persons within her community who passed judgment on this young man. The "calling out" of the sin of the community represents a prophetic function of the sermon. Therefore, this sermon was both prophetic and pastoral.

As the congregational pastor developed the funeral sermon of this young man along the periphery of her ministry, her point of departure was comforting the family with whom she knew well. As a hospice chaplain, my point of departure is always the image of God in the life of the deceased, regardless of the way in which they lived or died. As I prepare a eulogy for someone I do not know very well, I ask myself the following questions as I reflect on the stories shared by the deceased's family and friends: In the life of the deceased, where do I hear God's love, grace, and mercy? What godly characteristics are evident in the life of the deceased? Then, how do I uphold these God-like qualities as an offering that honors the life of the deceased and the living God and comforts the congregation?

From an anthropological perspective, honoring the God-like qualities of the deceased comes from my understanding of the image of God, the *imago Dei*. In light of the *imago Dei* as bearing qualities that reflect God, I believe that everyone has God-like qualities. However, sometimes those qualities are obscured by the way in which we choose to live our lives. Fortunately, through God's love we can be restored in that our God-like qualities become less obscured in life. Salvation represents the restorative means by which we live today. This redemptive work of Christ signifies our freedom from the divine consequence of sin and gives us eternal life.

Even if clergy are unsure of the deceased's salvation, the task of the eulogist is to reveal the image of God within the life of the deceased independent of how obscure the light of God shone in his or her life. The image of God is the lasting legacy the deceased leaves behind as a witness to those of the gathered community. Oftentimes, a funeral sermon is too generic and not specific to the life of the deceased. Therefore, the funeral sermon does not adequately present the image of God in the deceased's life. But the type of eulogy I have proposed in these pages connects the Gospel with the deceased's life, character, and personality to reflect the *imago Dei*.

Throughout this book, I discussed how to develop eulogies that unearth the *imago Dei* of someone unknown. To do so, clergy must use pastoral care during pastoral visitations to gather information and homiletic methods for the actual development of the eulogy. Fortunately, these same techniques can be used for people known to the eulogist. Below I provide the eulogy of my Aunt Anne who died unexpectedly in May 2025. I use the same skillsets of pastoral care and homiletic method to develop an inductive eulogy. The eulogy is infused with personal knowledge of my Aunt as well as knowledge gathered by reading the obituary, specifically with regards to her travels.

Eulogy of My Aunt Anne

My favorite Aunt, Aunt Anne, died unexpectedly in May 2025. She died doing what she loved, traveling the world. I thank God I was there to say goodbye and provide pastoral support to my shocked and grieved family. That week in the ICU in Chicago was one of the worst weeks of my life. I have sat with hundreds of families as they removed loved ones from life support and yet nothing prepares you for your own family tragedy.

My Aunt Anne was like my second Mom. She was the first person outside of my immediate family to say, "I see you and I love you!" Her untimely death was heartbreaking. I had the heavy task of delivering her eulogy. I could not publish a book on eulogies without including the eulogy of my beloved, Aunt Anne. Anne Mae Morse, may you rest in peace.

The title of the eulogy is "Wisdom Is Her Name." The sermonic text is Proverbs 8:1-11; 32-35. The eulogy provides another example of funeral preaching using the character sketch, one of the approaches I discussed in Chapter 2. I compare Lady Wisdom to my Aunt Anne, using the personified description of Lady Wisdom as descriptors of my aunt. Where appropriate, I add details of my aunt's life to add vivid imagery to the characteristics of Lady Wisdom. Drawing from the practice of inductive preaching, I delay the full idea of my aunt being Lady Wisdom until the last line of the eulogy when I say, "When you tap into the ways of Lady Wisdom, you will find her legacy of love. This beautiful, Black woman named Anne. Anne Mae Morse is her name."

Eulogy: Wisdom Is Her Name

Proverbs 8:1–11; 32–35

The Gifts of Wisdom

Does not wisdom call
    and understanding raise her voice?
On the heights, beside the way,
    at the crossroads she takes her stand;
beside the gates in front of the town,
    at the entrance of the portals she cries out:
"To you, O people, I call,
    and my cry is to all who live.
O simple ones, learn prudence;
    acquire intelligence, you who lack it.
Hear, for I will speak noble things,
    and from my lips will come what is right
for my mouth will utter truth;
    wickedness is an abomination to my lips.
All the words of my mouth are righteous;
    there is nothing twisted or crooked in them.
They are all straight to one who understands
    and right to those who find knowledge.
Take my instruction instead of silver
    and knowledge rather than choice gold,
for wisdom is better than jewels,
    and all that you may desire cannot compare with her.
"And now, my children, listen to me:
happy are those who keep my ways.
Hear instruction and be wise,
    and do not neglect it.

Happy is the one who listens to me,
    watching daily at my gates,
    waiting beside my doors.
For whoever finds me finds life
    and obtains favor from the Lord,

In the text this morning that was read for your hearing, we are introduced to the Wisdom literature of the book of Proverbs. In chapter 8, the writer of Proverbs personifies wisdom. Personification is when we attach human traits to ideas, objects, and other non-human entities. For example, justice is blind. Time marches on. Opportunity knocks. These sayings are all examples of personification in which we attach human traits onto ideas. Giving justice sight or the lack there of. Time marching as if time has legs. Opportunity knocking as if opportunity has hands.

Wisdom is personified as a beautiful woman. I might add a beautiful Black woman. If you allow me to use my sanctified, Holy Ghost imagination, wisdom is a tall, slender, beautiful Black woman, perhaps born in the Deep South, in the state of Alabama, coming of age in the 1960s during the Vietnam War and the Civil Rights Movement. A beautiful Black woman with milk chocolate skin, with a smile that could light up a room. A distinctive laugh that is contagious. A beautiful Black woman whose divine presence commands rooms because of her warmth and inviting spirit. A beautiful Black woman who is a consummate nurturer and soft place to land for those who need some extra love. A beautiful Black woman named Wisdom. Wisdom is her name.

Can you hear the voice of Wisdom in the text? If you close your eyes, can you see her as she instructs all who have ears to hear her voice? Lady Wisdom takes her stand by the gates, leading into the city, and cries out, simply saying, "I have given each of you instructions. These instructions are better than silver. I have given each of you knowledge. This knowledge is far better than gold." And we know that some of these instructions and knowledge have been given to us verbally, in the vein of our oral African traditions being passed down from generation to generation. Like that pecan pie recipe that was my absolute favorite. Lady Wisdom was so magnificent in the kitchen. She could just whip something up in a heartbeat. Sometimes when you ask Lady Wisdom, how did you make this? Lady Wisdom would just say, "Oh, you like that? Oh, I just threw something together. A little bit of this and a little bit of that." We recognize that other instructions and knowledge were not verbal, but they were modeled for us as we saw Wisdom move through life with a steady hand of unconditional love and extravagant grace.

What I love about Lady Wisdom is that she is not shy, but bold and courageous. Never afraid to tell you what she thinks or give some unsolicited advice, knowing that you probably need to hear it. Bold and courageous even when she is wrong. But the truth of the matter is Lady Wisdom is rarely wrong. She gives advice with the essence of God upon her lips. Because Wisdom knows God and knows God for herself. Lady Wisdom tells us time and time again. No matter what you're going through, you just have to trust God. Trusting God through the ups and downs of life. Co-creating life with God, building a life of love. This beautiful Black woman has 57 years of marriage under her belt. At 81, a lifetime of embodied wisdom, wisdom not from what she heard, but her own experiences marked by pain, joy, struggle, triumph, loss, and love. Lady Wisdom is familiar with the perplexities of life and the stories of what had happened was are not foreign to her. She shows us how to live with joy unspeakable, in spite of whatever the world throws our way. A beautiful Black woman named Wisdom. Wisdom is her name.

As we walk through this scripture, Lady Wisdom travels from the city gates, calling out wisdom to anyone who is willing to listen. Then, she shifts to explaining how she was there in the beginning of creation, co-creating with God. God and this beautiful, Black woman coming together to co-create from the beginning to eternity. Before the oceans were formed or the Islands of Key West, God gave birth to a beautiful, Black woman named Wisdom. Before the mountains were settled in place or the Great Smoky Mountains National Park, God gave birth to a beautiful, Black woman named Wisdom. As God gave the sea its boundary so the waters would not overstep God's command, and the foundations of the earth formed and the tectonic plates beneath the state of Alaska, Lady Wisdom reminds us that she is the wingman of God, this beautiful, Black woman named Wisdom.

She finally shifts her gaze from the co-creation of earth to that which she co-created, the apple of her eyes, her children. "And now, my children, listen to me: happy are those who keep my ways. Hear instruction and be wise, and do not neglect it. Happy is the one who listens to me, watching daily at my gates, waiting beside my doors. For whoever finds me finds life and obtains favor from the Lord." In these final words, Lady Wisdom instructs her children. I've given you all that I have. I've given you all that you need. Keep my ways and do not forget them. When you tap into the ways of Lady Wisdom, you will find her legacy of love. This beautiful, Black woman named Anne. Anne Mae Morse is her name.

BIBLIOGRAPHY

Andrews, Dale P. "Black Preaching Praxis." In *Black Church Studies: An Introduction*, ed. Stacey Floyd-Thomas et al. Abingdon Press, 2007.

Braxton, Brad. "Farewell to My Father: Reflections from a 'Preacher's Kid." http://www.theafricanamericanlectionary.org/pdf/preaching/TheDimensionsOfAFuneralSermon.pdf, 6-8, 2010.

Cunningham, Lawrence S., John Kelsay, R. Maurice Barineau, and Heather Jo McVoy. *The Sacred Quest: An Invitation to the Study of Religion*. 2nd ed. Prentice Hall, 1995.

King, Jr., Martin Luther. "Eulogy for the Young Victims of the Sixteenth Street Baptist Church Bombing." http://www.thekingcenter.org/archive/document/eulogy-four-girls-who-were-murdered-church-birmingham, 1963.

Lester, Andrew D. *Hope in Pastoral Care and Counseling*. Westminster John Knox Press, 1995.

Long, Thomas G. *Accompany Them with Singing: The Christian Funeral*. Westminster John Knox Press, 2009.

McClure, John S. *Preaching Words: 144 Key Terms in Homiletics*. Westminster John Knox Press, 2007.

McDonald, Nicole Danielle. 2024. "Homiletical Theory as a Pedagogical Paradigm." *Religions* 15, no. 8: 1009.

McMickle, Marvin A. *Where Have All the Prophets Gone: Reclaiming Prophetic Preaching in America.* The Pilgrim Press, 2019.

Mitchell, Henry H. *Celebration and Experience in Preaching.* Abingdon Press, 1990.

Mitchell, Henry H. *Celebration and Experience in Preaching.* Rev. ed. Abingdon Press, 2008.

Pew Research Center. "America's Changing Religious Landscape." May 2015. http://www.pewforum.org/2015/05/12/americas-changing-religious-landscape/.

Pew Research Center. "Religious Landscape Study." February 2025. https://www.pewresearch.org/religious-landscape-study/.

Thomas, Frank A. "The African American Funeral Sermon: Divine Re-Framing of Human Tragedy." http://www.theafricanamericanlectionary.org/pdf/preaching/FuneralsAndTheGoodNews.pdf.

Thomas, Frank A. *They Like to Never Quit Praisin' God: The Role of Celebration in Preaching.* The Pilgrim Press, 1997.

Tisdale, Leonora Tubbs. *Prophetic Preaching: A Pastoral Approach* Westminster John Knox Press, 2010.

Webber, Randall C. *A Balm in Gilead: Eulogies of comfort.* Jeffersonville, Indiana: BK Royston, 2019.

Wherry, Peter. *Preaching Funerals in the Black Church: Bringing Perspective to Pain.* Judson Press, 2013.

ENDNOTES

INTRODUCTION

1 When referring to particular funerals, the names are changed for anonymity.

2 Brad Braxton, "Farewell to My Father: Reflections from a 'Preacher's Kid'," accessed January 2, 2016, http://www.theafricanamericanlectionary.org/pdf/preaching/TheDimensionsOfAFuneralSermon.pdf, 6–8, 2010.

3 Marvin McMickle, *Where Have All the Prophets Gone?: Reclaiming Prophetic Preaching in America* (Pilgrim Press, 2006), 2.

4 Dale P. Andrews, "Black Preaching Praxis," in *Black Church Studies: An Introduction*, Stacey Floyd-Thomas and others (Abingdon Press, 2007), 203.

CHAPTER ONE

1 Peter Wherry, *Preaching Funerals in the Black Church: Bringing Perspective to Pain* (Judson Press, 2013), 49.

2 Pew Research Center, "Religious Landscape Study," February 2025, accessed September 1, 2025, https://www.pewresearch.org/religious-landscape-study/.

3 Pew Research Center, "America's Changing Religious Landscape," May 2015, accessed December 10, 2015, https://www.pewforum.org/2015/05/12/americas-changing-religious-landscape/.

4 A brief introduction to funeral preaching is provided in my essay Nicole Danielle McDonald, "Homiletical Theory as a Pedagogical Paradigm," *Religions* 15, no. 8 (2024): 1009. Homiletical theory is used as a methodology for teaching preaching, as demonstrated by the instruction on preaching Christian funerals.

5 Ibid.

6 John S. McClure, *Preaching Words: 144 Key Terms in Homiletics* (Westminster John Knox Press, 2007), 40.

7 Ibid., 41.

8 Thomas G. Long, *Accompany Them with Singing: The Christian Funeral* (Westminster John Knox Press, 2009), 187.

9 Brad Braxton, "Farewell to My Father: Reflections from a 'Preacher's Kid'," accessed January 2, 2016, http://www.theafricanamericanlectionary.org/pdf/preaching/TheDimensionsOfAFuneralSermon.pdf, 6–8.

10 McDonald, "Homiletical Theory."

11 Ibid.

12 Ibid.

13 Ibid.

14 Randall C. Webber, *A Balm in Gilead: Eulogies of Comfort* (BK Royston, 2019), 81.

15 Martin Luther King, Jr., "Eulogy for the Young Victims of the Sixteenth Street Baptist Church Bombing," accessed January 3, 2016, http://www.thekingcenter.org/archive/document/eulogy-four-girls-who-were-murdered-church-birmingham, 1963.

16 Ibid.

17 Ibid.

18 Ibid.

19 Ibid.

20 Leonora Tubbs Tisdale, *Prophetic Preaching: A Pastoral Approach* (Westminster John Knox Press, 2010), 9–10.

21 Martin Luther King, Jr., "Eulogy for the Young Victims of the Sixteenth Street Baptist Church Bombing," accessed January 3, 2016, http://www.thekingcenter.org/archive/document/eulogy-four-girls-who-were-murdered-church-birmingham, 1963.

CHAPTER TWO

1 Thomas G. Long, *Accompany Them with Singing: The Christian Funeral* (Westminster John Knox Press, 2009), xvi.

2 Ibid., 16.

3 Ibid., 188–195.

4 Frank A. Thomas, "The African American Funeral Sermon: Divine Re-Framing of Human Tragedy," accessed January 2, 2016, http://www.theafricanamericanlectionary.org/pdf/preaching/FuneralsAndTheGoodNews.pdf, 2000.

5 Frank A. Thomas, *They Like to Never Quit Praisin' God: The Role of Celebration in Preaching* (United Church Press, 1997).

6 Brad Braxton, "Farewell to My Father: Reflections from a 'Preacher's Kid'," accessed January 2, 2016, http://www.theafricanamericanlectionary.org/pdf/preaching/TheDimensionsOfAFuneralSermon.pdf, 6–8, 2010.

7 Andrew D. Lester, *Hope in Pastoral Care and Counseling* (Westminster/John Knox Press, 1995), 62.

8 Lawrence S. Cunningham, John Kelsay, R. Maurice Barineau, and Heather Jo McVoy, *The Sacred Quest: An Invitation to the Study of Religion*, 2nd ed. (Prentice Hall, 1995), 79–80.

9 Henry H. Mitchell, *Celebration & Experience in Preaching*, rev. ed. (Abingdon Press, 2008), 12.

10 Ibid., 13.

11 Ibid., 20.

12 Ibid., 20.

13 Ibid., 22.

14 Ibid., 23.

15 Ibid., 23.

16 Mitchell, 33.

17 A brief explanation of these strategies is provided in the essay "Homiletical Theory as a Pedagogical Paradigm" by Nicole Danielle McDonald, published in the peer-reviewed journal *Religions*. Homiletical Theory is used as a methodology for teaching preaching, as demonstrated by the author's instruction on preaching Christian funerals.

18 Henry H. Mitchell, *Celebration & Experience in Preaching* (Abingdon Press, 1990), 101.

19 McDonald, "Homiletical Theory."

20 Wherry, *Preaching Funerals in the Black Church*, 51.

21 Ibid., 51.

22 John S. McClure, *Preaching Words: 144 Key Terms in Homiletics* (Westminster John Knox Press, 2007), 62.

23 McDonald, "Homiletical Theory."

24 Ibid.

25 A sample inductive funeral sermon is in Chapter 5, the eulogy of my Aunt Anne, Anne Mae Morse.

26 McDonald, "Homiletical Theory."

27 A version of the eulogy written by Nicole Danielle McDonald is published in the chapter titled "In Remembrance: Saying Good-bye and Honoring a Legacy" in the book, *A Balm In Gilead: Eulogies of Comfort.* The eulogy emphasizes the importance of remembrance rituals to assist

the grieving of the gathered community. The names in all sermons have been changed to protect privacy.

28 I am not Irish. However, the patient was of Irish ancestry. MacDonald is a well-known Irish last name. Since my last name is McDonald, the spouse joked about the possibility of me being Irish in one of my pastoral visits.

29 Henry H. Mitchell, *Celebration & Experience in Preaching*, rev. ed. (Abingdon Press, 2008), 20.

30 Ibid., 23.

CHAPTER THREE

1 Merriam-Webster Dictionary, s.v. "theodicy," accessed January 25, 2016, http://www.merriam-webster.com/dictionary/theodicy.